Frank Field

Inequality in Britain:
Freedom, Welfare and the State

'No one who has engaged in the formulation of
schemes for improved income maintenance would
deny that it is hard to gain acceptance for them.
The abolition of slavery was not easy either.' Ronald
Henderson, *Australian Quarterly*, Winter 1980.

FONTANA PAPERBACKS

First published by Fontana Paperbacks 1981
Copyright © Frank Field 1981

Set in Monophoto Plantin

Made and printed in Great Britain by
William Collins Sons & Co. Ltd, Glasgow

To my brother John

Contents

Preface

A number of people have helped in the production of this book. Much of the reworked data appearing on the following pages were assembled by Bob Clements, Paul Hutt and Bob Twigger. Kay Andrews collected together for me copies of all the relevant Beveridge papers. In addition she commented upon the draft manuscript and both challenged and strengthened the argument. To all four, and in particular Kay Andrews, I owe a large debt of gratitude.

I am also grateful to the services provided to me by the House of Commons Library and to my secretary, Joan Hammell, for all her work on the manuscript. Any errors which remain are, sadly, my responsibility.

FRANK FIELD
Birkenhead
October 1980

Key to Abbreviations

Throughout the text and footnotes, any reference to the Royal Commission is a reference to the Royal Commission on the Distribution of Income and Wealth. All other Royal Commissions are referred to in full. All *Hansard* references are to the House of Commons *Hansard*. House of Lords *Hansard* are referred to in full. Elsewhere the following abbreviations stand for:

BIM   British Institute of Management

BLUE BOOK TABLES   Data on the distribution of income published annually in the CSO's National Income and Expenditure 'Blue Book' as well as in Economic Trends, drawing on information from a number of sources including the FES and the SPI.

BUPA   British United Provident Association

CIS   Counter Information Services

CPAG   Child Poverty Action Group

CSO   The Central Statistical Office, co-ordinating office and headquarters of the Government Statistical Service.

DE   Department of the Environment

DHSS   Department of Health and Social Security

FES   The Family Expenditure Survey, an annual survey

of expenditure, income and other characteristics of households, covering some 11,000 addresses each year.

FIS   Family Income Supplement

GHS   The General Household Survey, an annual survey documenting the social conditions and characteristics of some 15,000 households.

IDS   Incomes Data Services

NI   National Insurance

PEP   Political and Economic Planning

SBC   Supplementary Benefits Commission

SPI   The Inland Revenue's annual sample Survey of Personal Incomes which provides extensive information on the distribution of income before and after tax, and analyses the components of income and marginal tax rates.

Two major changes in the welfare state have occurred during the period under study. Child benefit has replaced family allowances and child tax allowances, and national assistance, which was established as the safety net in the welfare state in 1948, was superseded by supplementary benefit in 1966. The latter change was really only a change in terminology.

Introduction

Inequality in Britain is not just another book about the poor. Certainly the poor feature in it, but so do the rich. Poverty must be seen in relation to the total wealth of the community and, thus, this book is concerned with the fundamental question of the overall distribution of income and wealth in Britain. It is written, moreover, on two assumptions: first, that poverty is linked to other forms of disadvantage – not in the sense of a cycle of deprivation, but rather as part of a cycle of inequality – and, second, this poverty trap can be broken when people have adequate financial resources to sort out their own lives. The welfare reforms proposed here are directed to this objective and the aim of the book is twofold. The first is to provide readers with a comprehensive text which will hopefully persuade them to look at old issues in a new light. The second is to outline a manifesto, and one which a Labour government might implement.

Those who propose major reforms must also address themselves to a central political issue. What effect would their proposals have, if carried out, on the degree of freedom enjoyed by the community? *Inequality in Britain* takes the view that wherever possible people should make their own decisions about their lives, and not surrender their rights to third parties. But this assertion amounts to nothing more than empty sloganizing unless measures are taken to ensure that all citizens have the resources to choose from a full range of options. For too long the equation of choice with freedom has been monopolized by the Tory Party.

In fact, as *Inequality in Britain* demonstrates, practical, or what this book calls home-made socialism is an essential means of extending freedom. Over the past twenty years or so the goal of socialism has increasingly been seen as equality, and left-wing consensus on this priority is a testament to Anthony Crosland's evangelical skill. One of Crosland's most important successes was to hijack the Labour Party and convert it into a vehicle which saw 'socialism [as being] basically about equality'.[1] In contrast, *Inequality in Britain* returns to those older traditions of the Left which espouse freedom as the main objective, and greater equality as a means to that end.

This distinction between means and ends is not just of academic interest. The Croslandite view has had a profound effect on Labour policies, many of which are now coming under attack. Ironically, it is those Croslandites who have left the party because of Labour's espousal of equality at the expense of freedom who are the most virulent in their criticism. Yet the contested policies are the very ones which follow inevitably from putting maximum emphasis on equality while believing that somehow freedom will thereby be increased.

The re-establishment of freedom as the central goal of British socialism leads inevitably to a questioning of the assumption that socialism is axiomatically bound up with extending centralized power. That Croslandite values can often lead unintentionally to greater rather than less state power, and at the expense of ordinary individuals and not just of the rich, has been best exposed by one of Crosland's younger and most distinguished disciples. David Marquand has put this argument in the following terms:

The great engine of social-democratic redistribution has always been tax-financed public expenditure. High taxes, social democrats have assumed, would take resources away from the rich; high social spending would distribute them to the poor. But if the state takes my money away from me to give it to someone else, my freedom is thereby diminished. If those to whom it is given receive it in the form of cash, which they can spend as they like, and if there are a lot of them and only a few of me, there may well be a net gain in freedom. If they receive it in the form of services, in the direction of which they have no say and over the allocation of which they have no control, there will be no gain in freedom, though there may still be a gain in equality.[2]

Marquand makes a valid point, but he does not go on to make any distinction between those areas, such as education, where the somewhat old-fashioned line of raising taxation and redistributing this in the form of services is still an appropriate and legitimate goal, not least in terms of extending freedom, and a policy of cash redistribution as advocated in this book. That said, and recognizing the importance of Marquand's criticism, his argument is far from complete. *Inequality in Britain* argues that both socialism and freedom can be served by redistribution of cash in four ways: first, a cash redistribution from the state to individuals; second, a cash redistribution over an individual's lifetime so that forty years' earnings are spread over a seventy- to eighty-year period; third, a cash redistribution from rich to poor; and fourth, a cash redistribution from men to women.

But another argument is also involved here. Socialists need to reflect on the period since 1945 and ask what lessons are to be learnt about the performance of the state's machine. One lesson from the past thirty years is the inability (thank God) of the state to regulate effectively much of what each of us gets up to. By ignoring the lessons of the technical limits on what the state can effectively do, Labour directly assists the Tories who have not been slow to capture public fears of state power and to fashion them into a campaign for a nightwatchman state.[3] *Inequality in Britain* argues that to accept that state power is much more limited than has often been appreciated by the Left is not an argument for decrying all state action. Rather, it is a plea for concentrating the resources and expertise of the state machine on what it is able to do. One area where the state should be involved – and can, thankfully, be effective – is in helping to determine the distribution of income and wealth.

The central message of this book – the link between socialism and freedom – is developed by way of an essay on what determines an individual's standard of living. Obviously a person's wage or salary cheque is important as are the whole range of social security benefits. But this is an incomplete analysis and *Inequality in Britain* introduces the idea that there is not one, but five welfare states – each of which has to be considered if we are to gain a fuller understanding of what constitutes welfare,[4] and much of the book is concerned with how living standards are determined by means of each welfare state. The primary aim of any reform of welfare should be to ensure that all five welfare states combat rather than aggravate poverty and inequality. It is from this starting point that a major programme of welfare reform is advocated which will increase the power of those on or below average earnings.

To this end the first chapter is concerned with the total distribution of income and the poor's share in the wealth of the community. Discussion turns in the second chapter to how poverty has traditionally been defined. While the popular conception of poverty may well be one couched in absolute terms, social investigators for the past hundred years have always measured poverty in relative terms. Indeed, such an approach follows from the view outlined in Chapter 1, which places the poor within the total spectrum of Britain's income and wealth.

The third chapter reviews the main groups who find themselves poor at any one time and Chapter 4 examines the last attempt, Beveridge's, to implement a comprehensive anti-poverty programme in Britain. The failure of this scheme – which accounts for today's poor – is examined, as are the various stages where political pressure was applied to modify the scope of the reform. These major changes were not limited just to the adequacy and coverage of the benefits. One key part of the Beveridge proposals was the finance of the traditional welfare state. Chapters 5 and 6 look at this question in detail. They show how the Beveridge system of a tripartite funding never materialized. Chapter 6 looks at how the Exchequer contribution to the traditional welfare state is raised in a less and less progressive manner. The dockers' MP, Jack Jones, used to sing when marching through the Division Lobbies against pre-war welfare legislation, 'it's the poor that pays for the poor'. Chapters 5 and 6 show that this is largely true today.

Welfare in this book is defined as the provision of cash and services which help to determine the living standards of individuals and families. The way the tax base is being eaten away by the granting of tax allowances introduces the first of the other four welfare states. The granting of tax allowances reduces the tax liability of many taxpayers and is clearly a means of determining a person's welfare. Chapter 7 looks at the main provisions of the tax allowance welfare state. Increasingly, companies have been drawn into providing welfare benefits for their employees and Chapter 8 details the main form these benefits have taken and their growth over the past couple of decades. As with the tax allowance welfare state, the company welfare state acts as a way of increasing inequality rather than diminishing it. So, too, do the other welfare states – the welfare state resulting from unearned income, and the private market welfare state. These two forms of welfare provision are examined in Chapters 9 and 10.

The traditional benefit welfare state can only be effectively overhauled and extended if a total view is taken of Britain's five welfare states. Chapter 11 proposes a radical reform of all five welfare states. It is entitled 'Freedom First' because that is precisely what the aim of welfare should be and they are policies which will hopefully provide some of the main planks in Labour's next election manifesto. How realistic an aspiration this is is examined in the final chapter.

Contrary to popular myth, Labour in government has

never taken a comprehensive view of welfare, or even fully understood the workings of the traditional welfare state. This failure is now the more critical given the current government's policies for reducing the welfare of the poor. But despite the political advantage offered by the Thatcher government's actions, if Labour is to survive as a great political party, let alone win the next election, it needs to offer an alternative vision of a just society which will command new votes. The extension of freedom to the vast majority of the population by overhauling Britain's five welfare states offers an opportunity of a new coalition of votes for Labour. The book ends by discussing the sceptic's view that the party will fail to react positively to the suggestions made here. As Dr Johnson once remarked, 'the prospect of being hung in the morning concentrates the mind wonderfully.' This may well be a message for a Labour Party which at the last election gained the support of only 28 per cent of the electorate.

1. Poverty and Riches

Many people still think that poverty is a self-inflicted wound. While a recent EEC study showed that in Britain people were far more likely than in any of the other EEC countries to take this personalized view of poverty, this book puts forward an almost opposite view. Poverty is seen largely as a consequence of the current distribution of income and wealth in our society, and while particular individuals may escape from poverty by their own efforts, the structure of earnings and benefits ensures that other individuals will take their place. This chapter begins by looking at the distribution of income, and the extent to which the shares of the rich and the poor have changed over the past thirty years, before going on to examine the changing distribution of wealth. As well as examining changes over time in who owns Britain's wealth, a distinction is made between two types of wealth: that which affects a person's level of consumption and that which confers power over other people. This information will form the background for an examination of the traditional welfare state, the main function of which is to compensate for the maldistribution of income and wealth. It will also give an insight into the four other welfare states which will be examined in detail in later chapters.

Better - Consumption & production

Whose fault?

The most commonly accepted belief about poverty used to be that it was somehow inevitable, just like the air we breathe. This view has best been described by Noel Streatfeild who, when writing about events at the turn of the century, observed:

> It seems strange today, but that some children were hungry was accepted, as wet weather is accepted. I can remember my mother helping to serve soup, which could be bought by the needy for a penny a jug, and hearing her say: 'Fill that jug up to the top, and give the children extra bread, that family never has enough to eat.' ... Neither the tradesmen who provided the materials for the soup, nor the ladies who served it, appeared to think it wrong in a rich country that families could be in such want that they would queue for a pennyworth of soup. There was nothing wrong with the people of that date, they were just as kind-hearted and easily moved as we are today, it was that the way they thought was different; poverty was something that happened – just as people were born cripples, you helped them, but you could not expect to cure them – indeed there were many who supposed that it would be upsetting God's purpose if you did.[1]

I believe people are just as kind as Streatfeild described them. More importantly, they are willing to consider major structural reforms if these are presented in a relevant manner with a sense of moral purpose. I believe it possible to mobilize the goodwill which exists, to build the support for a total restructuring of Britain's five welfare states. But while most people in Edwardian England accepted poverty as part of the Divine Order, a new creed has now gained widespread support. The massive rise in national income has led large sections of the electorate to conclude that not only must everyone have reached an acceptable minimum standard of living, but that in achieving this society must have necessarily become more equal. Underlying this belief is a static view of income distribution which holds that any gains for those at the bottom end must inevitably be won at the expense of those at the top. In fact, a growing national income can lead, and probably over the past couple of decades has led to a widening gap between those at the bottom and the top.

Growth has also affected people's political values to the extent that it has reinforced the 'blaming the victim' syndrome: those who fail to keep up with the march in rising living standards are held to be morally responsible for their state. The poor are therefore caught in a pincer movement. On the one hand there is reluctance to accept the existence of 'real' poverty, while on the other hand, because of the rise in national income, those who accept that poverty does exist in Britain today are likely to view it in terms of personal and sometimes moral failure.

The importance of this 'blaming the victim' syndrome can be seen from the 1976 EEC-wide survey on people's attitudes to poverty. The results of the UK poll were at considerable variance with the overall EEC findings on the causes of poverty. In Italy and France, for example, the most common response was to put the blame at society's door. However, the UK findings show a high degree of personalized blame.[2] The main results show:

Cause of poverty	In agreement in UK
1. Laziness	45 per cent
2. Chronic unemployment	42 per cent
3. Drink	40 per cent
4. Ill health	36 per cent
5. Too many children	31 per cent
6. Old age and loneliness	30 per cent
7. Lack of education	29 per cent
8. Lack of foresight	21 per cent
9. Deprived childhood	16 per cent

In contrast, a central theme of this book is that the present distribution of our income and wealth makes it inevitable that large numbers of people will be poor in relation to the rest of the community and that poverty cannot be viewed as separate from the issue of who gets what in our society. Long ago R. H. Tawney warned of the dangers for the poor in undertaking studies of those on low incomes in isolation from other groups. In an inaugural lecture to the Ratan Tata Foundation, Tawney emphasized that an understanding of poverty required much more than a study of the poor themselves. He told his audience that the researcher 'would be wiser to start much higher up the stream than the point he wishes to reach', and then went on to warn that 'what thoughtful rich people call the problem of poverty, thoughtful poor people call with equal justice the problem of riches'.[3]

Income distribution

Students wishing to start 'higher up the stream' can be thankful to the Royal Commission on the Distribution of Income and Wealth (hereafter referred to as the Royal Commission) for bringing together a great deal of information on what is known about the current distribution of income and wealth in the UK. The Royal Commission collected together the three main sources of data on the distribution of personal incomes in this country: the Survey of Personal Incomes (SPI); the Family Expenditure Survey (FES); and the combination of the two, which goes under the title of the Blue Book Tables, and which is the 'only official statistics compiled solely for the purpose of presenting information about the distribution of personal income'.[4]

Turning to the Blue Book data, which are presented in Table 1, we find a remarkable stability in the share of total income going to the bottom 50 per cent of income earners, and this holds true whether one looks at the distribution of income before or after tax. In 1949, the bottom 50 per cent of the income distribution picked up 23·7 per cent of total personal incomes. By 1976/7 the total share of income had risen by 0·4 per cent to 24·1 per cent of the total of personal incomes. The position is not significantly altered if we look at the distribution of income after taxation. In 1949, the bottom 50 per cent of the distribution gained 26·5 per cent of the total and by 1976 they again gained 0·4 per cent more, giving a total of 26·9 per cent of total personal incomes. The extent to which this is altered by the payment of welfare benefits is examined in Chapter 6.

What of the income shares going to the top end of the distribution? Here the Blue Book data give a somewhat different picture. Taking income before tax we find that the share going to the richest 10 per cent has fallen from 33·2 per cent in 1949 to 26·2 per cent in 1976/7. Although this is a significant reduction, the table shows that most of this redistribution took place before the 1970s and, as we have seen, the bottom 50 per cent have not gained from this redistribution. It is that total part of the population who came between the top 10 per cent and bottom 50 per cent who have benefited most from the movement away from the top income groups. A similar trend is apparent in the post-tax distribution of income.

One way of illustrating how the problem of poverty is bound up inextricably with the problem of riches is to show how much more income high-income earners receive compared with those on low income. In any large-scale industrial society there will always be differences in incomes, but what is important is the ratio of these differences and particularly the gap between the top and the bottom. Amongst the highest paid directors in the UK (taking 1978/9 figures) were Lord Grade earning £195,208 from Associated Communications Corporation, R. R. S. Edgar with £132,000 from Hill Samuel, A. Stewart Moore with £110,750 from Gallaher, and C. Pocock with £109,634 from Shell, to name but a few.[5] At the other end of society are workers in what are called wages-council industries where the statutory minimum wages range from

Table 1 *Distribution of personal income – Blue Book,*
Percentage shares of total personal income received by given

United Kingdom

Quantile group (per cent)						Before tax income				
	1949	1954	1959	1961	1962	1963	1964	1965	1966	1967
Top 1	11.2	9.3	8.4	8.1	8.3	8.0	8.2	8.1	7.7	7.4
2-5	12.6	11.5	11.5	11.1	11.2	11.2	11.3	11.5	11.1	11.0
6-10	9.4	9.3	9.5	9.7	9.7	9.7	9.6	9.4	9.7	9.6
Top 10	33.2	30.1	29.4	28.9	29.2	28.9	29.1	29.0	28.5	28.0
11-20	14.1	15.1	15.1	14.8	15.2	15.4	15.5	15.2	15.2	15.2
21-30	11.2	12.4	12.6	12.5	12.6	12.6	12.6	12.5	12.6	12.6
31-40	9.6	10.5	10.7	10.8	10.9	10.9	10.9	10.7	10.9	11.1
41-50	8.2	8.9	9.1	9.3	9.2	9.1	9.2	9.3	9.1	9.1
51-60		7.4	7.5	7.8	7.6	7.5	7.4	7.5	7.4	7.7
61-70		5.3	5.9	6.0	6.0	6.0	5.9	5.8	6.0	6.0
71-80	} 23.7	} 10.3	4.4	4.6	4.4	4.4	4.3	4.5	4.7	4.8
81-90			} 5.3	} 5.4	5.1	5.3	5.2	} 5.6	3.4	3.4
91-100									2.2	2.2

Quantile group (per cent)						After tax income				
	1949	1954	1959	1961	1962	1963	1964	1965	1966	1967
Top 1	6.4	5.3	5.3	5.5	5.7	5.3	5.3	5.2	5.1	4.9
2-5	11.3	10.6	10.5	10.5	10.6	10.6	10.7	10.5	10.0	9.9
6-10	9.4	9.4	9.4	9.1	9.3	9.5	9.9	9.7	9.4	9.5
Top 10	27.1	25.3	25.2	25.1	25.6	25.4	25.9	25.4	24.5	24.3
11-20	14.5	15.7	15.7	15.0	14.9	15.3	16.1	15.6	15.3	15.2
21-30	11.9	13.3	13.2	13.0	13.1	13.0	12.9	12.9	13.0	13.0
31-40	10.5	10.3	11.2	10.9	11.2	11.2	11.1	11.0	10.8	11.0
41-50	9.5	9.1	9.9	9.8	9.6	9.3	8.8	9.3	9.6	9.7
51-60		8.3	7.2	8.2	8.3	8.2	8.0	7.9	7.8	7.7
61-70		6.4	6.6	6.1	6.0	5.8	5.6	6.2	6.8	7.1
71-80	} 26.5		5.2	5.7	5.6	5.3	5.1	4.8	5.0	4.9
81-90		} 11.6	} 6.0	6.2	5.9	6.5	6.5	6.9	7.2	7.1 {
91-100										

*Old basis: excluding mortgage interest payments etc.
*New basis: including mortgage interest payments etc.

£36 for a full week's work in hairdressing through thirty-five other wages-council industries to a top minimum wage of £52.50 for workers in non-food shops. Yet despite the parity of these rewards, underpayment of the legal minimum appears to be a growing problem.[6]

Another way of examining these differences is to look

National Income and Expenditure, 1949 to 1976/7
quantile groups, and supplementary statistics; before and after tax

Income unit: tax unit

1968/9	1969/70	1970/1	1971/2	1972/3	1973/4	1974/5	Old basis* 1975/6	Old basis* 1976/7	New basis* 1975/6	New basis* 1976/7
7·1	7·0	6·6	6·5	6·4	6·5	6·2	5·6	5·4	5·7	5·5
10·7	10·8	11·1	11·0	10·8	10·6	10·6	10·4	10·5	10·7	10·8
9·3	9·4	9·8	9·8	9·7	9·7	9·8	9·8	9·9	9·8	9·9
27·1	27·2	27·5	27·3	26·9	26·8	26·6	26·6	25·8	26·2	26·2
15·4	15·5	15·9	15·9	15·8	15·6	15·8	16·1	16·1	16·1	16·2
12·9	13·0	13·2	13·2	13·1	12·9	13·1	13·1	13·3	13·2	13·3
11·0	11·0	10·9	11·0	11·0	11·2	11·0	11·4	11·1	11·5	11·1
9·4	9·4	9·0	9·2	9·2	9·3	9·3	9·3	9·2	9·2	9·1
7·6	7·6	7·4	7·4	7·5	7·5	7·6	7·6	7·5	7·5	7·4
6·2	6·1	5·9	5·9	5·9	5·8	5·8	5·9	6·0	5·8	5·9
4·7	4·7	4·6	4·5	4·8	4·7	4·6	4·6	4·7	4·5	4·6
3·4	3·3	3·1	}5·6	5·8{	3·5	3·6	3·6	3·8	3·5	3·7
2·3	2·2	2·5			2·7	2·6	2·6	2·5	2·5	2·5

1968 9	1969 70	1970,1	1971 2	1972 3	1973 4	1974 5	Old basis* 1975 6	Old basis* 1976 7	New basis* 1975 6	New basis* 1976 6
4·6	4·7	4·5	4·6	4·4	4·5	4·0	3·6	3·5	3·9	3·9
9·8	9·7	10·0	10·0	9·8	9·8	9·7	9·4	9·4	9·7	9·7
9·2	9·2	9·4	9·5	9·4	9·3	9·5	9·3	9·5	9·5	9·6
23·6	23·6	23·9	24·1	23·6	23·6	23·2	22·3	22·4	23·1	23·2
15·5	15·6	15·9	15·9	15·8	15·5	15·8	15·8	15·9	15 8	16·0
13·1	13·3	13·3	13·4	13·2	13·2	13·2	13·4	13·4	13·5	13·3
11·5	11·4	11·2	11·3	11 2	11·2	11·4	11·4	11·3	11·3	11·3
9·7	9·7	9·5	9·4	9·5	9·5	9·4	9·7	9·4	9·6	9·3
8·1	8·1	7·8	7·8	8·0	7·8	7·8	7·9	7·9	7·7	7·7
6·6	6·7	6·5	6·4	6·5	6·4	6·4	6·5	6·8	6·3	6·6
5·3	5·2	5·2	5·1	5·5	5·4	5·3	5·4	5·2	5·3	5·1
}6·6	6·4	6·6	6·6	6·8{	4·2	4·4	4·4	4·6	4·3	4·5
					3·2	3·1	3·2	3·1	3·1	3·0

Source: Royal Commission, Report No. 7, Tables A1 and 2.

at the share of total income gained by different groups as opposed to individuals. The data for 1976/7 show the top 20 per cent of income earners gaining more than the share going to the bottom 60 per cent of the income distribution. Not all this bottom 60 per cent would think of themselves as poor, or indeed should be defined as poor, but before turning to how poverty has been defined in the post-war period it is necessary to look at the change in distribution of wealth over time.

Wealth distribution

As one of Britain's five welfare states arises from the unequal distribution of wealth, we need to look carefully at the different ways wealth is measured and in particular whether the widespread belief in a steady erosion of the capital of the very rich is borne out by the facts. Thanks to the work of A. B. Atkinson and A. J. Harrison we can present a picture of the changing distribution of wealth in Britain since 1923. While the authors warn us about reading too much into the figures over time, they are, nevertheless, the best data available and we can see from Table 2 two important trends in the ownership of wealth since the

Table 2   *Distribution of wealth, 1923/72**

	Share of total wealth					
	1923	1938	1960	1964	1970	1972
Top 1 per cent	60·9	55	33·9	34·5	29·7	31·7
2–5 per cent	21·1	21·9	25·5	24·1	23·9	24·3
6–10 per cent	7·1	8·1	12·1	12·8	15·1	14·4
11–20 per cent	5·1	6·2	11·6	12·9	15·8	14·5
20 per cent	94·2	91·2	83·1	84·3	84·5	84·9

* Economically independent population, England and Wales. The estimates for 1923 and 1938 are not wholly comparable with those for 1960 and later.

Source: A. B. Atkinson and A. J. Harrison, *Distribution of Personal Wealth in Britain,* CUP, 1978.

1920s. The richest 1 per cent has seen a significant reduction (almost a halving) of their wealth holdings, but this loss has been cornered by the next richest 19 per cent in the wealth stakes. The top 2 to 5 per cent increased their share slightly, the following 5 per cent more than doubled theirs, while the richest wealth holders between 10 and 20 per cent almost trebled their share. The total share of wealth going to the wealthiest 20 per cent of the population declined from 94·2 per cent to 84·9 per cent. As one group of researchers observed, 'This is hardly a dramatic decline over a period of fifty years. By the beginning of the 1970s, the poorest four-fifths of the population owned just 15 per cent of all personal wealth.'[7] And the very limited extent to which wealth has been redistributed has been best expressed by Professor Atkinson in one of his earlier works in which he concluded his study by saying: 'It seems therefore that what redistribution there has been is not between rich and poor, but between the very rich and the rich.'[8]

What pattern of wealth distribution is shown by more recent data? In its reports, the Royal Commission listed five ways by which the distribution of wealth is measured – Series A to E – and it is important that we look at each series, for they show a range of concentration of wealth with the result that each series is used by different protagonists in the political debate to prove their point. The five series are also important for this book as later we begin to make a distinction between the different kinds of wealth, looking carefully at the concentration of wealth or property which gives power over other people, as opposed to property which enhances self-esteem and dignity.

Series A are estimates based on estate duty returns and the wealth holdings of the population are calculated in the following way: those who die in any one year are treated as a sample of all wealth holders and these data are adjusted for differential mortality rates by sex, class and age. The difficulty with this approach is that many estates never come to the notice of the Estate Duty Office, either because they are too small to be subject to tax or because their owners have managed to steer them around the tax system through employing one of the many tax avoidance and evasion schemes.

Series B assumes that the 20 million missing persons who do not appear in the estimates own no wealth at all. As we can see from Table 3, this suggests an even more striking concentration of wealth in a few hands than is suggested by Series A. The top 1 per cent corners 23·2 per cent of wealth compared with 17·2 per cent. The top 5 per cent own almost half while the top 10 per cent own almost two-thirds of all wealth. Moreover, the way the Royal Commission present these data is not without its own significance. While the Royal Commission consider the top 1, top 5, top 10 and top 20 per cent of wealth holders separately, the remainder of the wealth-holding population was grouped together. Could there be a more powerful way of summing up the inequality in wealth than to refer to the *bottom* 80 per cent of the distribution?

The third way in which the distribution of wealth is presented is in Series C. This attempts to adjust Series A by assuming that we all have some wealth, even if it is not declared. The technical way by which this series is compiled is by using personal sector balance sheets which are the record of wealth held in private hands. The result of including not only missing persons but also some of the missing wealth is that the share of the top 1 per cent of the population unexpectedly rises to 24·4 per cent in 1975 and that the bottom 80 per cent to 23·3 per cent, with those in the 'middle' enjoying a reduced share.

Series D on wealth distribution is compiled from Series C but includes occupational pensions as a form of wealth. Series E takes Series D and includes in the analysis the value of state pension rights. The effect on the overall distribution of wealth by these adjustments can be seen in Table 3 which presents the distribution of wealth in 1975. The effect of making these adjustments is that the share of the top 1 per cent drops from 24·4 per cent in

Table 3 *Distribution of personal wealth, 1975. Series A–E*

Quantile group	Population included in Inland Revenue estimates (Series A) %	Total adult population (aged 18 and over), assuming that persons not covered in Inland Revenue estimates have no wealth (Series B) %	Excluding occupational pension rights (Series C) %	Including occupational pension rights (Series D) %	Including state pension rights (Series E) %
Top 1 per cent	17·2	23·2	24·4	21·0	13·9
Top 5 per cent	35·0	46·5	46·1	41·3	28·8
Top 10 per cent	47·3	62·4	59·9	55·0	39·5
Top 20 per cent	63·3	81·8	76·1	71·9	53·8
Bottom 80 per cent	36·7	18·2	23·3	28·1	46·2

Series A and B are for UK. Series C, D and E apply to GB.
Source: Royal Commission, Report No. 5, Tables 28, 41 and 43.

Series C to 13·9 per cent in Series E. A similar reduction
is recorded for the share of wealth going to the richest
5 per cent of the population. Thereafter the reduction
is far less marked, the share of the richest 20 per
cent of the population declining from 71·9 per cent in
Series D to 53·8 per cent once state pensions are taken
into account. Even so, the bottom 80 per cent of the
population's share of wealth rises from 23·3 per cent in
Series C to 28·1 per cent in Series D and to less than
half of all measurable wealth in Series E.

For the theme of this book it is important to include
both occupational and state pension rights for we are
concerned both with the means by which living standards
are safeguarded when people are unable to work and with
the mechanism by which wealth can enhance the living
standards of some members of the working community.
But as one of the welfare states we are examining is that
which results from unearned income, it is important to pay
special attention to those forms of wealth which give rise
to an income irrespective of the status of the wealth holder.
For example, occupational and state pensions are only paid
to people of certain ages, and while participants to an
occupational pension scheme have recently been prevented
from trading in their contributions, the membership of
such a scheme can be used in certain circumstances as a
guarantee of other loans. In contrast, state pension rights
cannot be used as a guarantee for raising capital. Other
forms of wealth holdings have none of these restrictions
on them and therefore it is important to look in a little
more detail at Series C, and particularly at changes in the
distribution of wealth between different groups since 1974
when the basis of the Series was changed to cover the whole
of the UK.

Here we find the share of the most wealthy 1 per cent
rising from 22·5 per cent in 1974 to 24 per cent in 1977.
Similar increases are shown for the top 5 per cent of wealth
holders in each of the years. The reason for this slight
increase in inequality of wealth holdings can be found in

the types of assets held by the very rich. The dramatic decline in the share of the top wealth holders between 1971 and 1974 was due not to redistributive policies adopted by the incoming Labour government but to the collapse of the stock market. The poor certainly gained nothing from the declining share prices that reduced the book value of the assets of the wealthy. Similarly, as share prices began to recover after 1974, the share of the richest wealth holders once again increased.

Conclusion

On the basis of the data produced by the Royal Commission and the Inland Revenue we can say that inequality in wealth is much greater than that of personal income. In respect of wealth, therefore, the poor have more in common with the majority of the population than they do with respect to the distribution of income. Only a very small minority of the population is not dependent on selling its labour or receiving benefits for its income, well-being and livelihood. Many people in the middle reaches of the distribution of personal income are reduced to a fairly low level of income soon after the breadwinner is unable to work, and this applies to those entering retirement if they are not covered by a generous private pension scheme or (as we are calling it in this book) provision from the company or the private welfare state.

The Blue Book Tables showing the stability of the share of personal income going to the bottom 30 per cent may give the impression that the poor are a static group. This is not so. While it is true that some people remain poor for all or most of their lives, others experience poverty only when they lose their ability to earn a living. Most people's lives are subject to three vulnerable periods – when they are responsible for children, when they are prevented from working, and when they retire. The extent to which these vulnerable periods are countered by payments from one of the four welfare states is the subject-matter of much of this book. But before looking at the extent of welfare we need to examine how poverty is defined.

2. What Is Poverty?

What is meant when we talk about poverty in Britain in the 1980s? In answering this question this chapter begins by reviewing the way Charles Booth and Seebohm Rowntree defined poverty for their respective pioneering studies. We shall see that both of them thought of poverty in relative terms; in other words, that the standard of living of the poor was not absolute but related to the general living standards of the community. We shall also examine their calculations and show that Rowntree inaccurately gauged the relative income level needed for children compared to adults. As the Rowntree calculations form the basis for Beveridge's work, which itself formed the basis of the modern welfare state, these calculations are not only of academic interest. The second part of this chapter will show that this underestimation of the needs of children results automatically in an underestimation of the number of poor families in Britain today.

In the beginning

The two social investigators who pioneered modern poverty studies in Britain were Charles Booth and Seebohm Rowntree. Both defined poverty in relative terms and this is a tradition followed by investigators right up to Peter Townsend in his recent *Poverty in the United Kingdom*.[1] All these writers have accepted that the living standards of the poor are not set in absolute terms through time, but are related to and revised as the general standard of living increases. Adam Smith expressed these views in the following terms:

> By necessaries, I understand not only the commodities which are indispensably necessary for the support of life but whatever the custom of the country renders it indecent for creditable people, even the lowest order, to be without. A linen shirt, for example, is strictly speaking not a necessity of life. The Greeks and Romans lived, I suppose, very comfortably though they had no linen. But in the present time ... a creditable day-labourer would be ashamed to appear in public without a linen shirt, the want of which would be supposed to denote that disgraceful state of poverty.[2]

'Modern' poverty studies begin with Charles Booth for, as his biographers, the Simeys, have commented, his 'most striking innovation was his invention of the Poverty line'. The Simeys went on to observe: 'His definition of poverty was perhaps the first operational definition in the social sciences, "operational" in the sense that it provided the means whereby the truth or falsehood of his provisional hypotheses could be tested experimentally.'[3]

Booth set out his definition of poverty in 1887: 'By the word "poor", I mean to describe those who have a fairly regular though bare income, such as eighteen or twenty shillings per week for a moderate family, and by "very poor", those who fall below this standard, whether from chronic irregularity of work, sickness, or a large number of young children.'[4]

So we see that such phrases as 'the poverty line', 'at' and 'below the poverty line', became common currency in the paper which carried the first results of Booth's enquiry. A year later, in a second publication, Booth made it plain that he was not seeking an absolute definition of poverty. The classification of those who were poor and very poor was determined by the popular opinion as expressed by his interviewers who had the job of classifying families. That poverty was a relative concept for Booth can again be seen from a key passage in his second paper. Families are defined as 'very poor' when their means are insufficient 'according to the normal standard of life in this country'.[5]

The idea that poverty could be defined independently of the society in which the investigation was being carried out is to be found in Seebohm Rowntree's first work. That he adapted this approach owes something to the political circumstances in which he was operating. Rowntree faced a different task to that of Booth, who had initiated his survey to undermine the propaganda of a newly formed socialist organization, the Social Democratic Federation (although, ironically, the results confirmed what Booth had thought of as the SDF's wild allegations about the numbers of poor in London).[6] Rowntree's purpose was to investigate the extent of poverty in a reasonably prosperous English city, and to counter any charge that his findings might exaggerate the extent of poverty he constantly emphasized that his was a minimum subsistence approach.[7] Writing at the beginning of his first report he made a distinction between primary and secondary poverty. Families living in primary poverty were those 'whose total earnings are insufficient to obtain the minimum necessaries for the maintenance of merely physical efficiency.'[8] Secondary poverty was thought of in terms as those 'Families whose total earnings will be sufficient for the maintenance of merely physical efficiency were it not that some portion of it is absorbed by expenditure, either useful or wasteful.'

Rowntree went on to recall that 'before we can arrive at any estimate of the numbers of those who are living in "primary" poverty in York, we must ascertain what income is required by families of different sizes to provide the minimum food, clothing, and shelter needful for the maintenance of merely physical health,' adding, 'expenditure needful for the maintenance of mental, moral or social sides of human nature will not be taken into account at this stage of the enquiry. Nor in thus estimating the poverty line will any account be taken of the expenditure for sick clubs or social insurance. We will confine our attention at present simply to an estimated *minimum* necessary expenditure for the maintenance of merely physical health.'

How Rowntree set about the task of calculating this minimum income consistent with 'merely physical health' need not concern us here.[9] What is important, however, is that most of the criticism of Rowntree's approach centres on the belief that his expenditure patterns, consistent with determining a poverty-line income necessary for merely physical efficiency, were unrelated to the lifestyles of most working-class families. Ironically this was initially true, but in the opposite way to that implied by his critics. Rowntree's attempt to produce a subsistence definition of poverty resulted in minimum income levels substantially *above* that obtained in reality by many working-class families. The only person, as far as I have been able to establish, who noticed this was Professor A. L. Bowley who wrote:

the food ration used by Mr Rowntree as a minimum is more liberal, so far as can be judged, than that obtained by the majority of working-class even in Europe in 1913, and by the great bulk of the unskilled and agricultural labourers in England before the end of the fall in prices in 1895. The human race has got along on a standard below this minimum, though it may have been hungry, with imperfect health, a high death rate and a low standard of efficiency. It is very important to recognize this, for it has come as a surprise to many people to learn that a large proportion of even an advanced population is insufficiently fed ... since they have not realized that the diet obtainable from wages of unskilled labour has in past times been generally too low for the work of a high grade, and that the poor and the working-classes were really interchangeable terms in past generations.[10]

Throughout his life Rowntree returned to the question of what constituted poverty. His first revisions were made in 1914 (although not published until after the end of the First World War) and this study was characteristic of those which were to follow. Considerable emphasis was placed on the supposed scientific determination of a minimum income and on the fact that this minimum was, if anything, set at an unbearably low level. At the same time, favourable adjustments were made to the level of a poverty-line income so ushering in the concept of relative poverty. Rowntree, like so many social reformers, found it necessary to dress radical findings in Conservative clothes.

With his revisions to the poverty line in 1914, Rowntree began to be much more open about setting minimum living standards that corresponded to those that were current in working-class households. And while the 1914 revisions reduced the food requirements of the minimum diet (as if anticipating Bowley's criticism) a new category of personal sundries was added. Commenting on this new entry Rowntree observed that 'personal expenses ... are quite necessary.' The items covered by personal sundries can be divided under three heads. A sum was included for compulsory national health insurance. Also included were trade union subscriptions, or additional subscriptions to sick clubs since these 'may almost be regarded as necessary, and this holds good of tram fares to and from work.' In addition, there were a number of other claims

varying in their urgency – such as expenditure for newspapers, for incidental travelling, for recreation, for occasional presents for the children, for beer and tobacco, subscriptions to churches or chapel, burial and sick clubs for the wife and children, and the multitude of small sundries such as stamps, writing materials, hair cutting, drugs etc. – for which it is difficult to make an accurate estimate, but some outlay upon which it is impossible to avoid.

To cover all the items under the heading of personal sundries, Rowntree calculated 'we cannot possibly allow a sum of less than five shillings a week' for a family of five.[11] Five shillings a week (or 25p) may seem little enough in today's money but it amounted to a considerable part of the earnings of manual male workers at the time. The only survey of pre-war earning was carried out in 1906 and 25p equalled about one-fifth of median male earnings.

In the 1930s, Rowntree carried out a major revision of his definition of poverty by developing a human needs scale, and this was used for calculating the levels of poverty in York in his 1936 survey.[12] One major change in Rowntree's definition of poverty was to extend the number of personal items in the budget. Sums were added to cover the cost of a wireless, together with a holiday, books and travelling. But again, the dietary requirements were tightened, and Rowntree based this latter change on the report of the advisory committee to the Ministry of Health which was published in 1931.[13]

Penalizing children

These minimum subsistence levels were computed not only for the purpose of carrying out social surveys but also to influence policy. Very early on in his career Rowntree openly made his definition of poverty a relative one (although, as we have seen, Bowley suggested that the very first definition was set at a level above the living standards of many working-class families). At the same time, he consistently emphasized its subsistence aspect, no doubt in an attempt to persuade the public to take seriously his findings on the extent of poverty. A 'catch-22' situation was reached, however, when these minimum subsistence levels were recalculated by Beveridge.

In *Social Insurance and Allied Services* – published in 1942 as the blueprint for the traditional benefit welfare state – Beveridge's calculations placed the emphasis squarely on the word minimum although this was not a point emphasized in the report, or in its subsequent massive publicity launch. A detailed analysis of Beveridge's calculations has been presented elsewhere[14] but here it is important to note the political context within which Beveridge was carrying out his work.

As Beveridge began preparing his report, politicians increasingly saw the whole exercise as important in raising morale for the war effort; it was crucial that people had something better to look forward to after the cessation of hostilities. As two of the major war historians commented:

> There existed, so to speak, an implied contract between Government and people; the people refused none of the sacrifices that the Government demanded from them for the winning of the war; in return, they expected that the Government should show imagination and seriousness in preparing for the restoration and improvement of the nation's well-being when the war had been won.[15]

Hence Beveridge was able to write early on in his report that the 'determination of what is required for reasonable human subsistence is to some extent a matter of judgement; estimates on this point change with time and generally in a progressive community, change upwards.'[16] Beveridge went on to argue that Rowntree's primary poverty scale would 'be rejected decisively by public opinion today', and asserted that insurance benefits would have to guarantee a minimum standard of living related to Rowntree's human needs scale'. However, careful reading of the Beveridge proposals shows a minimum income level which was below the 1936 Rowntree standard. The rate proposed by Beveridge for a single man and woman was 55 per cent

and 66 per cent respectively of Rowntree's human needs
scale. The rates for single pensioners ranged from 75 per
cent to 91 per cent of the Rowntree rates for a single man
and a single woman to 95 per cent for a married couple.
Beveridge's calculations for children were substantially
more generous than Rowntree's, although, as we shall see,
it is questionable whether Beveridge's relativities were
correct. Beveridge's minimum income level for a family
with one child was only 86 per cent of the Rowntree scale,
but for families with more than three children the Beveridge scale was more generous.

When Beveridge's report was published at the end of
1942 it was greeted with immense enthusiasm.[17] One is
left wondering, however, whether there would have been
such acclaim if the unsuspecting public had been aware
of just how much less generous was the proposal for a
minimum income level in the post-war world – or had it
been aware that wartime inflation would not be taken
into account fully when computing the revised benefit
levels. Beveridge's calculations were all based on 1938
prices. The cost of living rose by 73 per cent during the
decade before the 1948 National Assistance Act was
brought into operation, yet the minimum income scales
were revised by only 56 per cent.

In Chapter 4 we shall look in detail at how the Beveridge
Plan was pared down. Here it is important to note that
not only did the Attlee Government fail to compensate
fully for wartime price rises (thereby cutting in real terms
the Beveridge-proposed minimum income levels) but also
took the opportunity to make further revisions which
counted against households with children. Beveridge set
the rate for children at 58 per cent of the single person's
rate. This relativity was not maintained in the National
Assistance Board's scale rates for 1948. Although the
benefits for children were age-related, their average value
was less than 44 per cent of the single person's rate. A
child had to be aged over sixteen for the relative value of
its benefit to be greater than that advocated by Beveridge

in his flat rate proposal. These cuts in the scale rates for children were made even though there was growing evidence at the time when Rowntree and Beveridge undertook their calculations that they had underestimated the relative needs of children.[18]

These miscalculations had two serious consequences. First, as the relative needs of children to adults were, and still are, underestimated, the poverty-line income for households with children is similarly affected, with the result that fewer families are classified as poor than is in fact the case. This is an important point to keep in mind when looking at the official figures on the numbers of poor as we do in a moment. More importantly, however, these calculations have reduced the relative income of poor families compared to other low-income households. The effect of this has been to make poverty that much more acute for families with children. Their increased deprivation is illustrated by two sets of information. The first set of evidence comes from official surveys on the relative living standards of households on supplementary benefit. The second source of data comes from nutritionists.

The official survey on the sick and disabled (in 1972) and unemployed beneficiaries (in 1974) examined whether claimants had clothing which had brought their stocks up to the minimum level. Both surveys showed that households with children were less likely to own clothing stocks equal to the minimum rates. Forty-three per cent of single sick/disabled claimants without children had stocks of clothing less than the recommended level but this rose to 61 per cent of claimants with two or more children. The equivalent figures for unemployed claimants were 49 per cent and 76 per cent respectively. The surveys also reported on claimants who had fallen into debt since being on benefit. Again, there was a close correlation between borrowing and the presence of children in the household. The surveys also showed that the additional cash from borrowing was spent on food, clothing, heating and housing costs.

It is instructive to read these passages in conjunction with Rowntree's 1936 definition of poverty. Indeed, commenting on these findings the Supplementary Benefits Commission observed that 'The evidence presented ... regarding the standards of living of supplementary benefit recipients strongly suggests that the supplementary benefit scheme provides, particularly for families with children, incomes that are barely adequate to meet their needs at a level that is consistent with the normal participation in the life of a relatively wealthy society in which they live.'[19]

The second set of evidence about the adequacy of the children's rates in supplementary benefit is provided by nutritionists. Caroline Walker and Michael Church used 1975 National Food Survey data to examine the food purchases of different socio-economic groups. The total energy value of the food consumed and its monetary value were then used to calculate the number of calories obtained per penny. On the basis of this work, Walker and Church were able to challenge one very widespread belief about the consumption pattern of the poor. They suggested that their results showed that 'low income groups and large families tend to buy more efficiently than high income groups and small families.' Their second finding was based on spending the *whole* of the supplementary benefit allowance (for a five- to ten-year-old) on food, which again showed 'that the present supplementary benefit allowance ... is inadequate to cover the food needs of the largest eight- to ten-year-olds, even with the most efficient purchasing pattern.' And the authors added: 'since the requirements of many five- to ten-year-olds fall within the adult range, is it reasonable to pitch their allowance at only 33 per cent of an adult's?'[20]

The extent to which we underestimate the needs of children can be seen if we draw on any of the budgetary studies which have been undertaken since the end of the last century in Europe and the United States. These show that the cost of raising a child becomes equal to that of living as an adult at around the age of fourteen or fifteen. From then on, the needs of teenage children are seen to be greater than those of a single adult. This is not just because of the pressure of teenage culture. Dietary studies in the USA have shown that the cost of feeding a thirteen- to fifteen-year-old male teenager is 106 per cent of the adult rate, rising to 125 per cent for a male teenager between sixteen and nineteen. But it is when the total needs of children are taken into account, covering their clothing, personal care and recreation, as well as food, that one sees the full costs of maintaining dependants. The recent estimates given by the Community Council of Greater New York show that the relative costs of a child under one year old are put at a fraction under 33 per cent of the adult rate but this rises to almost 93 per cent for a twelve- to fifteen-year-old child and to over 112 per cent for a sixteen- to nineteen-year-old teenager. In comparison, the supplementary benefit minimum income levels are 63 per cent for a thirteen- to fifteen-year-old rising to only 77 per cent for a sixteen- to seventeen-year-old teenager. If the children's rates are measured against the single adult householder's allowance, the relativities are lower still, at 51 per cent and 61 per cent respectively.

Today's poverty

Circumstances have greatly changed since Booth coined the phrase 'the poverty line' over ninety years ago. But the poverty scales developed by Rowntree were adjusted by him to take account of rising living standards, and his 1936 scales were used by Beveridge in formulating what became in 1948 the National Assistance poverty line. Since then the scale rates have regularly been revised. The latest revisions are for November 1980. (See Table 4.)

Table 4 *Supplementary benefit rates, November 1980*

	Ordinary weekly rate £	Long-term weekly rate £
Husband and wife	34·60	43·45
Person living alone	21·30	27·15
Non-householder:		
aged 18 and over	17·05	21·70
aged 16–17	13·10	16·65
Any other person:		
aged 11–15	10·90	10·90
aged 5–10	7·30	7·30

Source: DHSS.

These benefit levels are called scale rates and from them it is possible to work out the poverty line or minimum income for households of different sizes. Everybody is eligible for supplementary benefit providing they are not in work and their total income from all sources is below their supplementary benefit entitlement. Claimants usually have their rent paid in full and their final income depends on whether they qualify for the ordinary weekly scale or the long-term scale rate. All pensioners drawing benefit qualify immediately for the long-term rate, whereas people below retirement age will qualify if they have been on benefit for one year and are not required to register for work. The exception to this rule is the unemployed, who are required to register for work and consequently have been consistently denied the long-term rate. So immediately we see there is not one poverty line in Britain, but two, and the gap between these rates has widened steadily since a difference was made in the rates in 1973, when the long-term rate was pitched at 10 per cent above the ordinary rate for a married couple. For a family with no children, the gap between the long-term and ordinary scale rate poverty line is now £8.85 a week or 26 per cent more than the ordinary rate.

For an unemployed man with a wife and two children, both under ten, paying the average rent of £7.40, the supplementary benefit allowance – or poverty-line income – is currently £56.60. In individual day-to-day terms it means that a married couple must cover 'all normal needs that can be foreseen, including food, fuel, light, the normal repair and replacement of clothing, household sundries (but not major items of bedding and furniture) and provision for amenities such as newspapers, entertainments and television licences' from an allowance of around £4.94 a day (after the rent has been paid) and are expected to keep their youngest child on £1.04 a day.[21]

Conclusion

The two pioneering studies of poverty in this country were carried out by Charles Booth and Seebohm Rowntree, and both defined poverty in relative terms. Beveridge then used the 1936 Rowntree standard for calculating the benefit rates for the new welfare state after the end of the war. But both Rowntree and Beveridge underestimated the relative costs of children and this has had two effects. First, as poor households with children receive relatively less income than do other childless people dependent on a poverty-line income from the state, the poverty of families with children is that much more severe. Second, this miscalculation has simultaneously minimized the official numbers of families in poverty; this needs to be borne in mind when we look, in the following chapter, at the official data on the numbers of poor.

3. The Poor

This chapter looks in a little more detail at the numbers and the people who are most likely to be poor today. People are poor in Britain in the 1980s not in terms of the original Rowntree definition of poverty, but in the sense that their incomes are too low in comparison with the living standards enjoyed by most of the population. The examination of the main groups in poverty, which takes up the first part of the chapter, pays special attention to the inadequate coverage and value of what are called national insurance benefits (such as unemployment benefit and old age pensions which are given free of means testing) which result in people being made dependent upon the safety net of means-tested supplementary benefits in order to bring their income up to the official poverty line. The second half of the chapter will be concerned with a critical examination of the view that the increase in the numbers of poor over the past thirty years can be explained by the use today of a relatively more generous definition of poverty compared to the one in use in 1948 when the National Assistance scheme came into existence.

Numbers on means tests

Taking the supplementary benefit scale rates as our definition of poverty, what does this tell us about the numbers of poor in post-war Britain?[1] Even though the 1948 National Assistance Act proclaimed: 'The existing

Poor Law shall cease to have effect,' the establishment of the post-war welfare state did not abolish poverty. Table 5 sets out the number of households drawing national assistance or, as it was renamed in 1966, supplementary benefit, for selected years since 1948.

The broad picture which emerges from this table is as follows. The number of households dependent on supplementary benefit has risen from a little over a million in 1948 to around 3 million in 1979. These figures do not measure the total number of persons whose living standards are determined by supplementary benefit payments. If dependants are included with the number of claimants the total rises to around 5 million.

While these figures are important for telling us the main groups in poverty they do not effectively illustrate the changing composition of the poor in the post-war period. For example, if we look at the number of households dependent on supplementary benefits in the post-war world we find that 63 per cent of them in 1948 were retirement pensioners. Thirty years later this proportion had dropped only three percentage points to 60 per cent. However, a totally different picture emerges if we look at the numbers dependent upon supplementary benefit rather than just the number of heads of households claiming benefit. In 1955 retirement pensioners and their dependants made up 61 per cent of persons dependent on national assistance payments. By 1978 this proportion had fallen to 44 per cent. In other words, if we take into account the number of dependants in households dependent on supplementary benefits we find that while only 39 per cent of the poor were below retirement age in 1955, their numbers have increased relatively faster than poor pensioners, so that today the poor under pensionable age account for 56 per cent of people dependent on supplementary benefits. A large part of this increase can be accounted for by the numbers of poor children, up from 309,000 to 1,048,000 in 1978 – an increase of a little over 62 per cent in the years since 1955. And this change in

Table 5 Numbers receiving supplementary benefit (in a week in November each year), selected years from 1948 (Great Britain)

	1948	1951	1961	1971	1974	1975	1976	1977	1978	1979
All supplementary benefits	1011	1462	1844	2909	2680	2793	2940	2991	2932	2850
All supplementary pensions				1919	1807	1679	1687	1738	1739	1720
Retirement pensioners and National Insurance widows aged 60 and over	495	767	1075	1816	1712	1586	1592	1636	1631	1630
Others	143	202	220	103	96	94	95	102	107	97
All Supplementary allowances				990	872	1113	1253	1253	1195	1130
Unemployed										
with contrib. benefit	19	33	45	129	73	135	654	128	93	80
without contrib. benefit	34	33	86	258	223	406	430	543	505	486
Sick and disabled										
with contrib. benefit	80	121	134	146	95	77	74	71	67	52
without contrib. benefit	64	98	133	159	165	165	169	158	156	155
NI widows under 60	81	86	58	65	42	30	28	22	22	19
Other one-parent families	32	41	76	213	245	276	303	309	322	306
Others	63	81	17	20	24	24	25	22	30	32

the face of poverty has occurred despite the fact that the measuring rod of poverty – the supplementary benefit rates – does, as we saw in the last chapter, underestimate the number of poor families with children.

The table gives us most of the main groups in poverty, but as Steve Winyard reminds us, it is important to make a distinction between the characteristics of the poor and the causes of poverty.[2] The reason why people are poor is either that they are unable to earn an adequate income, or that the welfare state fails to provide them with adequate resources when they are unable to work. It is important to look at each of these groups in a little more detail, for a rebuilt welfare state (see Chapter 11) will need to cater for the income needs of each of the main groups in poverty.

Groups in poverty

(i) The unemployed

In 1955 the average number of unemployed was around 180,000. Ten years later the average yearly number of people out of work stood at 306,000. From then on the upward climb in the jobless total quickened, the numbers out of work at the peak of each recovery being much higher than at the same point in the previous cycle. An average of 574,000 were without jobs in 1970 rising to 807,000 two years later. By 1975, in the wake of the oil price rises and the resulting world depression, the number of jobless jumped to over a million and by 1980 the monthly total exceeded 2 million.

Horrendous as the total is, it underestimates the number in search of work. The official figures are the result of the count of those workers registering for work, but we know that many of those who are unemployed but not eligible for unemployment benefit do not register as unemployed.

Likewise, an unemployed person is only eligible for supplementary benefit if his or her income is below the supplementary benefit level after taking into account other household income including the spouse's. The latest figures from the General Household Survey (GHS) suggest that about 300,000 to 350,000 people are unemployed, would like to work, but are not on the register.

These totals are a snapshot of the unemployed. They tell us about the numbers without work but say nothing of the length of time a person has been on the dole. An examination of the duration of unemployment shows that long-term unemployment is heavily concentrated amongst older workers. While there are large numbers of young people looking for work, few of them have been unemployed for long periods of time: 34·2 per cent of workers aged up to twenty years had been unemployed for over a month but less than three months, compared with 5·8 per cent of the same age group who had been unemployed for over a year. At the other end of the age scale, only 11·6 per cent of workers aged sixty to sixty-five had been unemployed for over a month but less than three months, compared to 55·7 per cent of those unemployed for over a year.[3]

Another way of looking at the burden of unemployment on different age groups is to study the median duration of unemployment. In January 1980, on average male workers had been unemployed for twenty-one weeks compared with seventeen weeks for women workers. However, for male workers under eighteen the average duration of unemployment was eight weeks rising to twelve weeks for those aged between eighteen and nineteen, to fourteen weeks for those aged between twenty and twenty-four years. On the other hand, unemployed workers aged between fifty and fifty-four had been on the register on average for thirty-five weeks, rising to forty-two weeks for those aged between fifty-five and fifty-nine and topping fifty-one weeks for those aged sixty to sixty-four. A similar pattern is found in the median duration of women workers. Young unemployed women workers aged under eighteen had been without jobs on average for eight weeks, rising to thirteen weeks for those aged between eighteen and nineteen, rising still further to sixteen weeks for those aged between twenty and twenty-four. For women unemployed workers aged between forty-five and forty-nine, their median duration of unemployment in January 1980 was twenty-three weeks, rising to thirty-one weeks for those aged fifty to fifty-four and topping forty-four weeks for those aged between fifty-five and fifty-nine.

Lower paid groups of workers are also more likely to experience repeated spells of unemployment. A recent GHS reports 4 per cent of professional workers, employers and managers as being unemployed during the previous twelve months compared with 15 per cent of the semi-skilled and unskilled workers. Moreover, while none of the former groups reported experiencing two or more spells of unemployment during this time scale, 3 per cent of the semi-skilled and unskilled manual workers had been so affected.[4]

Because low-paid workers are more likely to suffer unemployment more often, and for longer durations than other groups of workers, they are as a result more likely to exhaust their rights to unemployment benefit and become solely dependent on supplementary benefit. One of the trends in the post-war period has been the almost continual decline of unemployed workers being dependent exclusively on their national insurance unemployment benefit. This has been matched with an almost steady rise in the numbers of unemployed receiving supplementary benefits.

This growing tide of poverty is compounded by the numbers of unemployed who are drawing no benefit at all. In November 1978, of the total 1,331,000 registered unemployed persons, 280,000 were registered for work but on the day of the count were receiving no benefit at all, a jump from 254,000 in May of that year.[5] Only part of this total will gain benefit once their claim has been processed, and the non-claiming of benefit by some un-employed who are eligible to benefit must be largely responsible for the numbers of unemployed who are shown to be living below the supplementary benefit poverty line in the FES data. In 1974, 40,000 unemployed claimants together with 50,000 dependants were shown to be living on incomes below the supplementary benefit poverty line. Each year since 1974 has shown a steady increase in this total which stood at 150,000 unemployed claimants, to-gether with 140,000 dependants, in 1977.

(*ii*) *The old*

All the post-war poverty studies on the elderly have agreed on two findings. First, large numbers of people become poor as soon as they are old. Second, a significant pro-portion of old people are found to be living below the official poverty line. The extent of poverty amongst today's pensioners can be seen by looking at the numbers dependent upon means-tested assistance. At the present time there are 9·5 million pensioners of which a fraction over 2 million draw a weekly means-tested supplement in the form of a supplementary pension. As we shall see in the next chapter, Beveridge's original plan was to phase in adequate old-age pensions in the period up to 1956. Although more adequate pensions were paid in the earlier part of the post-war period than was originally set out in Beveridge's plan, the proportion drawing national assis-tance/supplementary benefit has been substantial although it has begun to fall over the past few years.

Depressing as these figures are, they underestimate the numbers of poor pensioners. The year 1972 witnessed the introduction of a national rent rebate scheme and in 1974/6 there was a deliberate policy of persuading pensioners drawing supplementary benefits to claim a rent rebate if this increased their total income. As a result, 90,000 pensioners were transferred to the rebate scheme, although it is now clear, with the changing eligibility for both schemes, that many of these pensioners would be better off reclaiming a supplementary pension. The immediate effect of the transfer was, however, to decrease the numbers and proportion of pensioners appearing in the supplementary benefit poverty figures.

There is a second reason why the numbers claiming supplementary pension are an inadequate gauge of the numbers of poor pensioners for it tells us nothing of those who are eligible but not claiming additional help. The most up-to-date information on pensioners with incomes below the supplementary benefit poverty line again comes from the FES data. These show 550,000 pensioners living on incomes below the official poverty line in 1974, rising to 740,000 in 1977.

(iii) Single-parent families

The Finer Report commented that three factors stand out in considering the present financial provisions in relation to the needs of one-parent families. They are the low level of income among working one-parent families compared with two-parent families, the lack of any worthwhile gain by combining part-time work with supplementary benefit payments, and the inadequacies and uncertainties of maintenance from an ex-spouse as a source of income. Single-parent families and the unemployed are the fastest growing groups in poverty. Between 1971 and 1976 the estimated number of one-parent families rose from 570,000 to three-quarters of a million, an increase of 32 per cent. Since then the numbers have continued to grow and it has been estimated that their present numbers stand at around 850,000 single parents bringing up one-and-a-half million children.[6] One explanation for this rise is the big increase in the numbers of divorced lone mothers.[7]

In 1976 about 300,000 single parents relied on earnings as their main source of income, and of these 70,000 were fathers. A recent study by the government shows working single-parent mothers to be at a double disadvantage. Not only are women generally low-paid but those single parents who were working earned even lower pay than other female workers. The study was of single-parent families drawing the Family Income Supplement (FIS), and as FIS is paid only to those on low wages, inevitably the sample was weighted to those on lower earnings. The survey found that the majority of FIS mothers were employed in three major industrial groups: miscellaneous services, distributive trades, and professional and scientific services – groups which employ large numbers of low-paid male and female workers. Most of the sample were engaged in traditionally female occupations of clerical, service or sales work. 'Average gross weekly earnings were £18.02 which compared with £26.04 for all full-time female workers at April 1974. Average hourly earnings for FIS mothers were 50.2p compared with 70.6p for all female workers.'[8] When asked their attitudes to their present job, low wages were cited as the main cause for dissatisfaction although four out of five of all FIS mothers said they would still prefer to work than stay at home.

Low income is compounded by additional living costs. For example, a survey carried out by what was then the City of Coventry's Children's Department showed single-parent families having three additional costs to meet. While it costs as much to run a home in terms of heating, lighting, cooking and mortgage for two parents as one parent, single-parent families have the additional costs of paying for household chores and, if working, the extra costs of prepared foods, as well as meeting child-minding bills. As one single-parent family observed, 'despite this lower income [compared to two-parent families] these families still have many of the expenses of two-parent families, and some additional ones.'[9]

Not surprisingly, therefore, large numbers find themselves dependent on supplementary benefit. In November 1978 there were 339,000 single-parent families living on supplementary benefit. This figure is 4 per cent higher than the previous year, whereas the number of two-parent families on supplementary benefit had fallen by 13 per cent to 196,000. Of the single parents, 324,000 were women and 15,000 men. Among the women there were 113,000 separated wives, 109,000 divorced women, 87,000 single mothers, 11,000 widows and 4000 prisoners' wives.[10]

The FES data suggest that the single-parent families are more likely to claim supplementary benefit than other groups of claimants, hence fewer were found to be among the very poorest. In 1974 it was estimated that about 20,000 single-parent families responsible for 50,000 children were living on incomes below the supplementary benefit poverty line. This total rose to 50,000 and 100,000 respectively a year later. In 1977, the total fell very slightly to 40,000 single-parent families together with 70,000 children living on incomes below the official poverty line.

(iv) Sick and disabled

Sickness, like unemployment, is a significant cause of poverty. Those on low incomes at work are least likely to have adequate resources to fall back on in periods when their earnings are interrupted. And yet the incidence of chronic sickness is much higher among the unskilled than among professionals. For example, unskilled men are three times as likely as professional men to report chronic sickness.[11]

Given that social classes 4 and 5 have more days off because of sickness than other groups, does the system of sick-pay schemes and sickness benefit favour these groups? The answer on both scores is 'no'. The GHS shows, for example, that manual workers are far less likely to be covered by sick-pay schemes than non-manual workers. Moreover, while there has been an improvement in coverage over the years since 1971, large numbers of workers in manual occupations are still outside the scope of an occupational or sick-pay scheme.

Whereas for some people sickness ends with the restoration of full health, for others it results in long-term impairment or handicap. Official government surveys have classified people as impaired if they lack all or part of a limb or have a defective organ or mechanism of the body. Handicapped people were classified as those among the impaired group who have difficulty in carrying out one or more of the activities associated with self-care.

A national survey carried out in 1968/9 by Amelia Harris and her colleagues found that there were just over three million impaired people aged sixteen and over living in private housing, including 1,128,000 who were very severely, severely or appreciably handicapped as far as self-care was concerned. These estimates have recently been brought up to date by Peter Townsend who added to the total 150,000 severely handicapped children aged under sixteen.[12]

The Harris survey also looked at the income of disabled persons and reported that between 35 and 40 per cent of disabled people surveyed were dependent on supplementary benefit. It also found that the disabled were, on the whole, poorer than the rest of the community, often housed inadequately, and restricted in their education and employment opportunities.[13]

A follow-up survey on the incomes of the disabled reported in the following terms: 'The best estimates of the numbers entitled to unclaimed supplementary benefit and unwilling to claim their entitlement, based on the results of this study, lie in the range of 50,000 to 70,000.'[14] This estimate was strongly disputed by the Disability Alliance who claimed that the figure of 70,000 was a rock-bottom estimate of the numbers living below supplementary benefit and the true figure was likely to be twice as high.[15]

If the Alliance's estimate is correct it would appear that the figures from the FES data may well underestimate by a considerable amount the numbers of disabled people living below the supplementary benefit poverty line. The FES grouped together those who have been sick or disabled for more than three months and showed that in 1974 20,000 families, covering 60,000 persons where the head of the household was sick or disabled, were living below the supplementary benefit level. This total stood at 40,000 and 70,000 respectively by 1977.

As a result of the introduction of the invalidity benefit scheme in 1971, the numbers of sick and disabled dependent on supplementary benefit have fallen. Nevertheless, there were still 223,000 on supplementary benefit in 1978, the majority of whom were not in receipt of invalidity benefit because they did not meet the contribution conditions. The non-contributory invalidity pension, introduced in 1975, has had virtually no impact on the numbers of non-insured sick and disabled on supplementary benefit. This is because it is paid at only 60 per cent of the contributory rate.

(v) Low paid

It is also important to look at those groups who are in poverty, but who, because they are unable to claim supplementary benefit, do not appear in the table. One such group is the low paid, who are usually defined as those earning less than two-thirds of average earnings. Taking this cut-off point, and using the New Earnings Survey data, and including only those working a full week, the following picture of low pay emerges. In 1970, 4·1 million workers earned less than two-thirds of average earnings even when their overtime pay is included. By 1979 this total stood at 3·2 million. Data excluding overtime earnings does not exist for the early years of the 1970s but, by 1979, if overtime earnings are excluded, the numbers earning less than two-thirds of average earnings rises to 3·7 million.

Low pay is heavily concentrated amongst women

workers and in certain industries. For every low-paid man there are two low-paid women workers, and if overtime is included then the ratio rises to three to one. Furthermore, although many workers find themselves low-paid either at the beginning or at the end of their working lives – or both – low pay is basically a structural problem. It is heavily concentrated in certain industries paying low wages regardless of the age, sex or race of the wage earner.

Taking a wage of £60 a week or less as a definition of low pay in 1979,[16] we see that 29 per cent of male workers in agriculture were earning less than this sum, as were 22 per cent of the distributive trades, 23 per cent in insurance and banking, 28 per cent in professional and scientific services, 26 per cent in miscellaneous services and 20 per cent in public administration. Given that there are many more low-paid women workers than their male counterparts, the roll call of industries employing low-paid women workers is obviously much longer. Again in 1979, 72 per cent of manual women workers in textiles were earning £60 a week or less, as were 77 per cent in clothing and footwear, 60 per cent in bricks, pottery and glass manufacture, 65 per cent in other manufacturing, 80 per cent in distributive trades, 83 per cent in professional and scientific services and 80 per cent in miscellaneous services.

The low paid make up the largest group below retirement age shown to be living on incomes below the supplementary benefit poverty line. In 1977, 230,000 households covering 640,000 individuals were so placed, a total which has risen by 75 per cent since 1974.[17]

(vi) Single women with aged dependants

The second group, most of whom do not appear in the supplementary benefit statistics, are single women with aged dependants. There is no exact record of the number of persons who have to give up work in order to care for an elderly relative at home, although some idea of the numbers can be gained from the 1966 Census. This shows that there were some 309,000 households comprising unmarried daughters with one or more parents of pensionable age, of whom 57,000 daughters were not economically active and a further 7,000 were out of work. More recently, the National Council for the Single Woman and her Dependants has suggested that 'There may be some 300,000 single women in this country who have taken upon themselves the task of caring for an elderly relative at home. Usually those relatives are one or both parents, but sometimes they stretch as far as uncles or aunts.'[18]

The most important consequence of giving up work to care for an aged relative is a drop in income, although there are a number of important social costs as well. A pilot survey carried out by the National Council in 1970 showed that of a group of eighty-five single women from its membership who had to give up work, only 4 per cent were financially better off. The majority suffered an appreciable drop in income: for 22 per cent this was up to £5 a week, for 28 per cent it was between £5 and £10 a week, and for 22 per cent the drop in income amounted to between £10 and £15 a week.[19] The invalid care allowance introduced in 1975 had little impact on the poverty described in this survey, for the benefit sets an income below the supplementary benefit level.

(vii) Poor in institutions

The third group whose numbers are largely excluded from the Table 5 are the poor living in institutions. Mainly because of the work of Ann Shearer,[20] the Royal Commission made estimates of the size of each of the four groups living in institutions who are likely to be poor. The first group concerns residents of old people's homes, but many of these, while poor, will appear as supplementary benefit recipients in the table. The second group living in institutions and liable to be poor are long-stay mental patients. In 1975 there were 106,428 long-stay patients in mental hospitals. A third group of poor people living in institutions are the residents in local authority hospitals for the mentally ill and mentally handicapped. In 1974 there were 4190 long-stay patients below the age of sixty-five and 21,380 aged sixty-five and over. The final group of poor people in institutions are those long-stay residents of hostels and lodging houses. A total number of such residents stood at a little over 28,000 in 1972 and most of these were shown to be living on very low incomes.[21]

What total do these figures give us of the numbers of poor in Britain today? The number of households dependent on supplementary benefit has risen from around 1 million in 1948 to almost 3 million today. Within these households live around 5 million people. To this group we need to add those who are living on incomes below the official definition of poverty – over 2 million in 1977. Yet even this total excludes those who are poor for part of the year but also have an annual income above the supplementary benefit level, as well as many of those living in institutions who never appear in the official statistics.

Real increase in poverty

Politicians have not been slow to argue that the increase in the numbers of poor is due to a more generous definition of poverty rather than an actual increase in the extent of poverty. For example, in the run-up to the 1970 General Election one minister was involved in a dispute about whether the poor had become relatively poorer during the period of the first two Wilson governments. The minister asserted that 'the supplementary benefit scale rates have been raised every year since the government took office. They are now, in real terms, 18 per cent higher than the

1964 national assistance scale. One result has been to increase the numbers of people drawing benefit by 600,000.'[22]

What was not in dispute was that supplementary benefits had risen in real terms – comparing their value at the time of each uprating. Indeed, in June 1959 a white paper entitled *Improvements in National Assistance*[23] was presented to Parliament which concluded that the government had been considering the position of those living on national assistance and had 'reached the conclusion that the time has come when it is right to move to a higher standard, so giving them [the poor] a share in the increasing national prosperity.' But the minister's argument that the numbers of poor had increased due to changes in the scale rates is only valid if their relative, as opposed to their real, value has been increased. Has this in fact happened?

We need, therefore, to consider a number of questions. In the first place we need to look at the extent to which the poor have always been protected against price increases. We then need to examine the extent to which the promise of giving the poor a fair share of the country's prosperity has been borne out by the facts. And lastly, we need to examine the extent to which the relative value of benefits has changed and the extent to which any such changes can account for the increase in the numbers of poor in the post-war world.

To what extent have the 1948 subsistence levels been revised to take account of increasing national prosperity? There is no doubt that if we take the period since 1948, the old national assistance scales (now the supplementary benefit rates) have risen faster than the rise in prices. From 1948 up to November 1979 the retail prices index (excluding housing costs) increased by 646·6 per cent. The increases in the scale rates over the same period of time are well over 1300 per cent.

Long-term claimants have been eligible for a higher rate of supplementary benefit since 1966. Since then, and up to November 1979, the benefit levels for a single person and a married couple on the long-term rates have risen by 426·7 per cent and 430·3 per cent respectively, while the retail prices index (again excluding housing costs) rose by 286·8 per cent.

Thus the living standards of the poor have been more than protected against price increases if we take the period as a whole since 1948. However, the practice has always been to award increases to compensate for price rises suffered since the last increase. But to what extent have benefit increases, well in excess of inflation, amounted to a real increase in the living standards of the poor, and have these increases matched the promise given in 1959 that the poor would have a fair share in the country's increasing prosperity? Two studies are relevant to this question.

The first piece of evidence comes from a major report from the National Institute of Economic and Social Research. Its authors were aware of the difference in the values of the supplementary benefit scale rates when measured against gross and net earnings, and so they reworked the data on 'an equivalent net income basis'. After doing so their results showed that 'the relative living standards of the poor appeared to remain approximately constant between 1953/4 and 1971, at about 49 per cent of the median for the fifth percentile and about 58 per cent for the tenth percentile.'[24] The study went on to report: 'this reflects the much sharper rise between 1953/4 and 1971 in the direct tax burden of median households (4·3 per cent of the gross income to 14·8 per cent) than for poor households (1·8 per cent to 3·2 per cent).' In their final comments the National Institute researchers observed: 'it is perhaps best to conclude that the evidence points to neither a significant deterioration nor an improvement in the relative income to the poor over this period.'

The Royal Commission undertook a similar analysis, which was reported in its *Lower Incomes* reference. It concluded that the rise in the living standards of the poor was due to a general rise in prosperity rather than to making the definition of poverty more generous. Taking 1961 as its bench mark, and measuring the period up to 1974/5, the Commission found that the average real income of the lowest three-tenths of family units increased by roughly 40 per cent, in line with the growth in the GNP of about 38 per cent.[25]

The third question under consideration is the extent to which the increase in the numbers of poor in the post-war period is due to the use of a more generous relative definition of poverty. There are considerable difficulties in answering this question and part of the complication arises from the different supplementary benefit scale rates in use. Earlier we noted that pensioner households are awarded what is called the long-term scale rate immediately, while other claimants draw the ordinary scale rate for their first year on benefit, except for the unemployed who continue to draw the ordinary scale rate no matter how long they are dependent on supplementary benefit. Moreover, these different scale rates need to be measured against gross and net (i.e. after stoppages) average earnings.

Once this is done three trends emerge. First, taking the ordinary scale rate and measuring it against gross average earnings of male manual workers, we find little change in the relative value of the national assistance/supplementary benefit rates over the period since 1948. For example, a married couple with two children drew a benefit of 39 per cent of gross average earnings in 1948 and one of 41·6 per cent in 1979. Even less change is to be found in the single person's rate which stood at 17·6 per cent and 18·6 per cent in 1948 and 1979 respectively. But even here there is one exception to this general trend. A married couple with four children drew a benefit averaged at 48·3 per cent in 1948 whereas an identical family's benefit was valued at 54·3 per cent of gross average earnings in 1979. These figures, however, disguise the small, but nevertheless important relative decline which has occurred since 1965, when again a married couple with four children drew a benefit averaged at 55·9 per cent of gross average earnings.

A second trend is apparent when the ordinary scale rate is measured against net earnings: here we see a relative improvement for all types of claimants. For a single person, the poverty-line benefit paid in 1948 was valued at 22·9 per cent of male manual average net earnings. By 1979 this had risen to 29·2 per cent. Yet most of the improvements occurred in 1965 when the benefit rose from a value of 26·5 per cent in the previous year to 29·4 per cent. Moreover, the ordinary scale rate benefits paid to most claimants reached their highest relative level in 1977 and have declined since then. The only exception to this trend is for households with two and four children where the relative value of benefits in 1979 was at a comparable level to that reached in 1965.

A third trend emerges on the long-term scale rates. These show a small improvement in the years since 1966 (when they were first introduced) when measured against gross earnings. For example, a married couple drew a benefit valued at 34·8 per cent of a gross average male manual worker's in 1969 and this had risen to 38·2 per cent by 1979. However, the biggest improvements occur when the benefit is measured against net earnings. There is a 6·7 percentage points increase for benefits paid to a married couple, and an increase of 8·1 percentage points to a household with four children.

Given this information, is the increase in the numbers of poor determined by the use of a more generous definition of poverty? The table on page 48 shows a fairly steady rise in the numbers of poor during the post-war period. But we have just seen that the most important change of the relative benefit levels against net earnings occurred after 1965. Clearly, the overall increase in the numbers of poor from the early years of the post-war period cannot be explained away in this manner. Even during the more recent years there are some unexpected trends to be considered. At the end of November 1973 there were 7,936,000 pensioners. By the end of 1978 this total had risen to 8,602,000. In the earlier year the number of supplementary pensions as a percentage of retirement pensioners was 23·2 per cent. If the same ratio had applied in November 1978 there would have been 1,996,000 supplementary pensions in payment compared with the recorded number of 1,720,000. And while it is true to say that the relative value of the retirement pension increased during this period – for a single person up from 26·1 per cent to 30·2 per cent – this increase was less than that recorded for the long-term rate of supplementary benefit which is automatically paid to all pensioners. Whereas the relative value of the retirement pension increased by 15·7 per cent in the period from 1973 to 1978, a 19 per cent increase is recorded in the relative value of the supplementary benefit pensioners measured against average net earnings. If relative increases in supplementary benefit rates are a cause of an increasing number of persons claiming supplementary benefit then one would have expected a swelling rather than a decrease in the total of pensioners drawing supplementary benefit since 1973. Even the transference of pensioner households to rent and rate rebates does not account fully for the decline in the number of claims for supplementary pensions.[26]

A further breakdown of the numbers claiming supplementary benefit in the period since 1973 shows that by far and away the biggest increase occurred among the unemployed. Various factors account for this increase, the most obvious possibilities being an increase in the numbers of unemployed, a change in the composition of the unemployed and an increase in the supplementary benefit rates relative to unemployment benefit rates. Throughout the period the flat-rate unemployment benefit was slightly above the short-term supplementary benefit level for a single person and a married couple, although this would not have been the case for most families with children. A further breakdown of the unemployed on supplementary benefit between those receiving a contributory benefit as well as those without a contributory benefit sheds some further light on the increase. In January 1974 the numbers of unemployed eligible for national insurance unemployment benefit stood at 71,000 rising to 108,000 in November 1978, while the numbers of unemployed ineligible for unemployment benefit rose from 229,000 to 593,000. Over this period, and even more so since the end of 1978, the numbers of school leavers who, by definition, have no national insurance contributions giving them a right to unemployment pay, as well as the numbers of unemployed who have exhausted their right to employment pay after being without a job for a year, increased as a proportion of the total unemployed. The increase in the numbers of unemployed receiving supplementary benefit over recent years is therefore almost certainly explained by the increase in the level of unemployment.

Conclusion

The numbers of poor have grown steadily during the post-war years although this has been a period of increasing prosperity. In 1948, 1 million households were drawing a minimum income from the state and today this total has risen to almost 3 million. If the number of people in these households is considered together with those living on incomes below the supplementary benefit poverty line, the total number of poor rises to 7 million and to a greater and greater extent poverty is to be found among families with children. Moreover, as we have seen, this increase in post-war poverty cannot be explained by the use of a more generous definition of poverty. Much more important reasons in accounting for the surging total of poor are demographic changes – the significant rise in the number of one-parent families, and the growing industrial collapse – which have resulted in an ever-increasing army of the unemployed. Given the highly inequitable distribution of unearned income, most people become poor when they are unable to work and some even earn their poverty. Because of age, sickness and family commitments, large numbers of people are unable to work, while others – such as the unemployed – are forced to be idle. Many of these groups are poor because of the failure of the traditional welfare state to provide an adequate income. What went wrong with the first attempt to establish a decent minimum income for everybody is the theme of the next chapter.

4. What Went Wrong?

things have progressively worse

The Beveridge proposals, which were greeted with a blaze of publicity and widespread public acclaim, appeared at the end of 1942. The main purpose of the plan was to abolish poverty – or Want, as Beveridge called it – but, as we have seen in the last chapter, far from abolishing poverty, the numbers of poor have steadily increased in the post-war world. Why is this?

To answer this question we will need to look in some detail at the introduction of the Beveridge scheme. The chapter begins by summarizing the findings of the inter-war poverty studies which formed a central backcloth to Beveridge's proposals and then goes on to show that even in the early papers which Beveridge wrote, and which later formed the basis of his major report, his conception of the social welfare state was inadequate to abolish poverty. These ideas were then further modified both by political and by Treasury pressure prior to their publication in 1942. There then followed three distinct phases in the public negotiations over the proposals, each of which led to major modifications of the scheme. Each modification itself meant that the proposals would be less effective in eradicating poverty. In the following chapter we shall then turn our discussion to a careful examination of the proposals Beveridge made for financing the social welfare state, and we shall see how regressive were the financial principles underlying the report and how these have been made even more regressive in the years following the publication of *Social Insurance and Allied Services*.

Poverty in the 1930s

The pioneering researches of Booth and Rowntree were followed by a bevy of similar studies throughout the inter-war years. Like Rowntree's research on the extent of poverty in York, these studies were by and large confined to university towns and, as the report from Political and Economic Planning (PEP) observed: 'the results emerging about the extent of poverty were uniformly gloomy.'[1]

Table 6 *Incidence of poverty before the Second World War*

Survey	Working-class households	
	Families in poverty %	Children in poverty %
London 1929	9·8	13·0
Merseyside 1929–31	17·3	24·5
Southampton 1931	21·3	30·0
Sheffield 1933	15·4	26·9
Miles Platting 1933	9·0	28·0
Plymouth 1935	16·5	—
York 1936	31·1	43·0
Bristol 1937	10·7	21·4
Birmingham (Kingstanding) 1939	14·0	31·0

Source: Poverty: Ten Years After Beveridge, PEP, 1952, p. 24.

Except for Rowntree's second survey of York, the studies adopted a roughly comparable definition of poverty. Their results showed that in many working-class districts almost one third of the children would be living in poverty, and the PEP study concluded: 'Having three or more children before the war in the working class was practically sufficient to guarantee poverty.'[2]

This finding on the link between children and poverty is an important one to remember when later we examine Beveridge's proposals on family allowances. It is equally important to remember the dates when most of the surveys were carried out. Over half of them were completed during the peak years of unemployment during the inter-war recession. When reviewing their findings Beveridge commented:

> from each of these [inter-war] social surveys the same broad result emerges. Of all the want shown by the surveys, from three-quarters to five-sixths, according to the precise standard chosen for want, was due to interruption or loss of earning power. Practically the whole of the remaining one-quarter to one-sixth was due to failure to relate earning to size of family.[3]

Enter Beveridge

We shall return to this point later to show that Beveridge's interpretation of the results of these studies was wrong (see p. 83), but in order not to break the chronological order of our discussion, we need to return to the middle of 1941 when the government announced the setting up of a committee which would merely review the various social insurance schemes which were then in existence. Beveridge, who was appointed chairman, was working at this time in the Ministry of Labour, and for reasons explained by his biographer, José Harris, had got under the skin of Ernest Bevin, the Minister of Labour in the Coalition government. Bevin was lukewarm about establishing the committee, and only became enthusiastic when he saw it as a chance of ridding himself of Beveridge. At this time Beveridge was busy trying to complete his inquiry into the manpower of the armed services. Indeed, throughout the autumn of 1941 the Beveridge Committee, as it was called, met infrequently, and Beveridge did not fully turn his mind to the issue of transforming the welfare state (a move clearly way beyond what the government had intended) until the end of 1941. Between December of that year and February 1942 he drafted two papers for consideration by the other civil servants who comprised the committee. The main ideas of the Beveridge Report were contained in these first major submissions.

At the beginning of *Social Insurance and Allied Services* Beveridge wrote:

> All the principal causes of interruption or loss of earnings are now the subject of schemes of social insurance. If, in spite of these schemes, so many persons unemployed or sick, or old or widowed are found without adequate income . . . this means that the benefits amount to less than subsistence . . . To prevent interruption or destruction of earning power from leading to want, it is necessary to improve the present schemes of social insurance in three directions: by extending the scope to cover persons now excluded, by extension of purposes to cover risks now excluded, and by raising the rate of benefit.

Furthermore, 'Abolition of want requires . . . adjustment of incomes, in periods of earnings as well as in interruption of earnings, to family needs, that is to say, in one form or another it requires allowances for children.'[4] We can see, therefore, that Beveridge had a clear conception of how to prevent poverty in the post-war world, so what went wrong?

First thoughts

In his first major paper on the reform of social welfare Beveridge wrote that the success of the scheme was dependent on the implementation of three other major reforms. The first of these was the introduction of the National Health Service; the second, the payment of children's allowances; while the third major policy was the maintenance of full employment (although Beveridge budgeted for an unemployment rate of 8·5 per cent). The Beveridge Scheme itself was built on a number of key principles, four of which are important to our discussion. These are that there should be a universal flat-rate benefit, that the benefit should itself be paid at an adequate subsistence level, that the range of benefits should cover all types of want and that benefits should be paid as long as want lasted.

Beveridge's preliminary papers for the committee show that in three very important respects the scheme failed to meet all the key principles Beveridge himself laid down. In respect of women, Beveridge failed to extend comprehensive coverage; a similar failure occurred in meeting the needs of non-industrially disabled people; and in his treatment of the question of rent, Beveridge failed to design a scheme which gave adequate subsistence benefits.

In respect to the rights of women, José Harris has observed that Beveridge was 'determined to give each category of woman a foothold in social insurance'.[5] In his first paper Beveridge considered the rights that should be given to what he terms 'unmarried wives'. In discussing this issue he wrote: 'This problem involves acute differences of opinion and principle. The state has already gone so far in recognizing the marriage in relation without marriage ... that it hardly seems possible to take the strict line ... that the unlawful marriage relation should not be recognized in the social security scheme at all.'[6]

However, when Beveridge came down to listing the groups to be helped by his scheme he proposed five insurance coverages for women:

1. Single women would contribute like men for a comprehensive insurance coverage.
2. Married women would be entitled to a special house-

wives' policy based on the insurance record of their husbands.

3. Employed married women would have the choice of relying on their husbands' insurance record or contributing to the scheme themselves.

4. Unmarried wives would be entitled to the coverage given to married women except that they would be denied a furnishing grant or a widows' pension.

5. Domestic spinsters – women working at home often caring for an aged relative – would be classified as as unoccupied person contributing solely in order to gain an old age pension.

Once Beveridge opened up discussion on these proposals he ran into considerable opposition. On the one hand there were those women's organizations, like the National Council of Women, who argued that the proposals did not go far enough, adding that married women should be paid housewives' allowances like a wage for an ordinary job. Similarly, one of the members of the committee, Mary Agnes Hamilton, campaigned for more generous treatment for the domestic spinster. Beveridge was 'dissatisfied' with his proposals for this group and 'assured Mrs Hamilton in March 1942 [that this group] "was very much in his mind"'.[7]

On the other hand there were those who were for a strict adherence to the insurance principle, and it was argued that in some important respects the provision being proposed by Beveridge for women undermined the insurance nature of the scheme. Here it is important to recall just how fundamental this concept was to the whole Beveridge proposals, for later on (see Chapter 11) we shall need to untie this Gordian knot in making plans for reforming the traditional welfare state. On the insurance principle Beveridge quoted the National Conference of Friendly Societies as well as the TUC's General Council in support of his view. Both these groups put forward three arguments in favour of an insurance-based welfare state. The first was that 'contribution irrespective of means is the strongest ground for repudiating a means test'. Second, to have a clearly defined social insurance fund will result in the contributors realizing 'that they cannot get more than certain benefits for certain contributions', while the insurance principle will teach contributors not to 'regard the state as the dispenser of gifts for which no one needs to pay'. Third, the insurance principle leads to clearly defined rights to benefit: 'Contribution provides automatically the record by which the insured person's claim to be qualified for any particular benefit can be tested.'[8] And if these were not conservative (although not unworthy) enough reasons for arguing for the insurance principle, Beveridge added one of his own for good measure. His plan for social security was based on a 'continuance of the tripartite scheme of contributions established in 1911. That scheme has been in force for thirty years and has won general acceptance.'[9]

Drafting the report

Slowly, but inevitably, the logic flowing from these beliefs began to undermine the scope of welfare provision for women originally proposed by Beveridge. Indeed, two months after the first complete draft of his report Beveridge had come to the conclusion that the giving of a separation benefit as part of the cover for married women in an insurance scheme was impracticable. He recommended instead that a deserted wife should have the right to means-tested public assistance and that the public body would pursue through the courts her right to maintenance from her husband.[10] Similarly, Beveridge began to change his mind on the correctness of proposing a separation allow-ance. As José Harris has acutely observed, this question 'placed Beveridge on the horns of a dilemma and brought into conflict two of his most deeply held beliefs about social insurance.'[11] On the one side, payment of benefit was the problem of paying a benefit to a 'guilty wife', for the scheme would be underwriting an event which was under the control of the individual. On the other side, if a benefit as of right was not paid then the wife would be subjected to a means test. This reasoning led Beveridge to conclude that in an insurance scheme a benefit for separation was unworkable.

By September 1942 he envisaged that such a benefit could only be paid in the case of divorce or legal separation. In his final report Beveridge proposed a Housewives' Policy to cover what he saw as the six marriage needs of a woman. One of these was in cases of separation: benefit would be paid to the women whom the husband failed to maintain after a legal separation or if the husband's desertion was publicly established. Here Beveridge proposed an adaptation of the widows' benefit, together with a separation benefit, a guardians' benefit and a training benefit.[12]

The second group which failed to gain a foothold into the social security system was the non-industrial disabled. The position of those made disabled at work was very different. Apart from war pensions, damages awarded by the courts were for centuries all that stood between an injured or deceased person's family and destitution or dependence on charity. A major change in this system came with the passing of the Workmen's Compensation Act of 1897, which introduced the idea of an employer being held liable for accidents to his workforce at work even though he was not personally at fault. The Act also provided cash benefits as of right and without first undergoing a test of means. The act stated: 'If in any employment to which this act applies personal injury by accident arising out of and in the course of employment is caused to a workman his employer shall ... be liable to pay compensation.' The act initially applied only to certain hazardous industries such as railways, factories, mines, quarries, engineering works or buildings over thirty feet high. In 1906 an additional act dealing with workmen's compensation extended the scheme to most people working under a contract of service or apprenticeship. The number of people covered by such schemes therefore rose from an estimated 7¼ million to some 15 million.[13]

While accepting that the system of workmen's compensation had conferred great benefits, Beveridge listed two major disadvantages. The first was that apart from mining industries, employer's liability insurance was not compulsory, with the effect that there was no certainty that compensation would be paid in all cases. Second, and partly as a result of this failure, the system's last resort was one of litigation. Commenting on the system, Beveridge concluded:

> the pioneer system of social security in Britain was based on a wrong principle and has been dominated by a wrong outlook. It allows claims to be settled by bargaining between unequal parties, permits payments of socially wasteful lump sums instead of pensions in cases of serious incapacity ... and over part of the field, large in the numbers covered, though not in the proportion of the total compensation paid, it relies on expensive private insurance. There should be no hesitation in making provision for the results of industrial accident and disease in future, not by a continuance of the present system of individual employer's liability, but as one branch of a unified capital plan for Social Security'.[14]

That Beveridge was totally concerned with industrial injury when considering the problems of disability can be seen from his preliminary paper 'Basic Problems of Social Security with Heads of a Scheme'.[15] The discussion of disablement in this document is exclusively concerned with industrial injury and the compensation which should arise from death resulting from industrial injury. Beveridge proposed that the larger invalidity benefit for permanent incapacity and death benefit should be given not according to the cause of incapacity but according to the industry in which the man was engaged, with compensation for engaging in a dangerous necessary trade. Beveridge believed there were three reasons why those who were industrially injured should be treated preferentially to other disabled people. The first was that many industries which were vital to the country involved considerable dangers to the workforce. Given the country's need for an adequate supply of labour to these industries, Beveridge believed it was necessary to assure workers that special provision was being made for the risks that they undertook. The second reason why those disabled at work should have preferential treatment was that the disability followed from a man acting under orders. The third was that it would be possible to limit the employer's liability at common law only if provision were made for the results of industrial accidents and diseases irrespective of the employer's negligence.

There are two reasons why Beveridge made no discussion of the congenitally disabled's needs. First, the issue was a much less important one then than today. One of the major gains of medical advance is to keep alive more people who would previously have died as a result of their disability at or shortly after birth. The second reason stems from Beveridge's insistence on an insurance scheme. How could people who had paid no contributions benefit from an insurance-based scheme? The problem was not insuperable for Beveridge could have argued that the right to benefit existed by way of the insurance record of the parents.

When the government came to consider its response to the Beveridge Report it did not challenge the restrictive scope for disability benefits. Rather, it changed the basis on which benefits should be paid to the industrially disabled. Beveridge argued for compensation based on loss of earnings. The complications of running such a scheme are obvious and have bedevilled payment of compensation through the courts. Establishing what a person would be earning if they had not been disabled at work at a time previously is far from an easy exercise. The government therefore decided that compensation should be paid not on loss of earnings but on loss of faculty. 'This decision marked a departure not only from the basis of workmen's compensation but also from the principle still followed today in industrial injuries compensation schemes in nearly all other countries.'[16] However, the government's radicalism on this point still left a growing number of disabled people outside the provisions of the main insurance scheme. As more and more congenitally disabled people survived birth and childhood and lived into adult life, this failure of Beveridge's original proposals became more and more obvious and important.

How a non-means-tested benefit should cover a claimant's rent was the other issue which faulted the Beveridge scheme from the very start. As we have seen in Chapter 2, a poverty- or subsistence-line income aims to cover all the necessary expenditure of a claimant. Rent is obviously one key element in this calculation.

The survey of working-class expenditure which the Ministry of Labour carried out in 1937/8 showed a wide divergence in the level of average rents in different parts of the country. In Scotland the average rent payment was 70·4 per cent of the mean for all industrial households, while in London the equivalent figure was 148·1 per cent of the mean.[17] These figures posed an acute dilemma for Beveridge. The scheme could propose three ways of dealing with rent payments. A flat rate could be given for all households although, as Beveridge accepted, no 'single figure can fit the true requirements even reasonably well'. Alternatively, the rent payments could be varied according to the region; however there were to be found wide variations in the level of rent payments within regions. The third method of covering rent payments was to adjust the level of benefit to take account of the actual rent paid. As one member of a special sub-committee which Beveridge established to consider the question of rent commented, 'this is the only way to overcome the difficulty created by the immense differences in the rents paid by working-class people.'[18]

The special sub-committee favoured a benefit level which would to some extent take into account the different levels of rent payments; yet in the end Beveridge opted for a flat-rate rent element. In an attempt to justify this position, Beveridge put forward two arguments. The first stemmed from his belief in an insurance system based on equal benefits for equal contributions. Beveridge did not reject variations in benefit according to rent level because of the administrative difficulties (although he was fearful that this would taint the scheme with some element of means-testing) but because he attached such importance to giving equal benefits for equal contributions. But as Rowntree retorted within days of the publication of the report, this argument ignored a more important inconsistency which was built into the scheme. The scheme proposed that a bachelor would receive a benefit of twenty-four shillings a week and would pay the same contributions as a married man who would draw a benefit of forty shillings.[19]

The second argument which Beveridge employed was that those paying higher rents were persons on higher income, and although this was a valid choice for people to make, it was not relevant when considering the payment of subsistence benefits. Again, this was an argument which Rowntree took apart. With a view to examining whether higher income groups paid higher rents, low rents being paid by poorer people, Rowntree re-examined a random sample of his 1936 interview schedules. From this he found that 52·6 per cent of households earning less than sixty-five shillings a week paid less than ten shillings rent while 47·4 per cent paid more. Of those earnings more than sixty-five shillings, 42·6 per cent paid less than ten shillings and 57·4 per cent paid more. 'If these figures may be taken as approximately applying to provincial cities generally, which I think they may, then I submit that they so largely disprove the theory that broadly speaking the poorer workers pay low rents and richer ones pay high rents that it may be discarded.'[20]

In the final report Beveridge 'provisionally' rejected the proposal to adjust benefit according to the actual rent paid by the claimant. In an article reviewing the prospects which the report held for abolishing poverty, Rowntree wrote of the flat-rate rent proposal: 'If this proposal is adopted, I think it would go far to defeat the central object of Beveridge's plan.'[21] Indeed, Rowntree wrote more prophetically than he could have realized, for Beveridge's failure to tackle effectively the rent question was seized upon by the government to help jettison the whole idea of subsistence-based insurance benefits.

Treasury cuts

From conception, the Beveridge scheme contained three fundamental flaws: the needs of women were not adequately covered, nor were the needs of all the disabled met, and the benefit paid to all claimants would not be adequate as some claimants' rent payments would not be covered in full. But, after Beveridge had completed his draft report, pressures were brought upon him to modify it in other important respects, so undermining still further the scheme's effectiveness to abolish poverty.

Initially, however, Beveridge was encouraged to review his plans which resulted in increasing the costs of the scheme as it stood. The Government Actuary, who was a member of the committee, estimated that on the draft proposals the Exchequer's expenditure on social welfare would be three times as high as it was in 1941, and that it would increase still further with the rapidly ageing population. In March 1942 Beveridge began a series of discussions with Keynes, then an economic adviser in the

Treasury, and later with other Treasury officials, on ways of limiting the scheme's cost. The first of these encounters led to Keynes ironically proposing to Beveridge that he should take into account wartime inflation; this, far from limiting the cost of the scheme, increased it in money terms by 25 per cent. However, Keynes suggested that Beveridge should make clear that he was not advocating frequent adjustments in the level of benefits to take into account rises in the cost of living. In addition, he proposed three other changes. He urged Beveridge to consider financing pensions out of current income rather than basing them on cumulative contributions. He told Beveridge that he was very keen on the proposed tax on dismissals, whereby employers would suffer heavy penalties for unfairly dismissing workers, and he urged Beveridge to be even bolder in his attack on the vested interests of the voluntary industrial insurance market.[22]

Taking into account the expected wartime inflation, the provisional cost of the scheme rose to £500 millions and it was at this point that the committee suggested three changes: that the proposed benefit levels should not be accepted as the final figures; that cuts should be made in maternity grants, dependents' benefits and rates paid to workers under twenty-one; and, more importantly, that full old age pensions should be introduced only over an extended period. Indeed, Keynes was soon writing to Beveridge expressing his alarm lest the scheme 'is being overwhelmed by the pensions part'.

In order to meet these objections Beveridge proposed a sub-committee to work on the financing of the scheme which would include Treasury representatives and Epps, the Government Actuary. Also, early in July 1942, Keynes returned to the attack on the pension proposals which he had previously described as 'the least interesting and least essential' part of the scheme. He suggested to Beveridge that while there should be no increase in pension levels for the first five years of the scheme, this should be followed by an annual increase of sixpence a week thereafter, and that during this transitional period pensions should be graduated according to the pensioners' contributions. At the end of July the Treasury officially offered the services of two of its economists, Keynes and Lionel Robbins, to help modify the financial aspects of the scheme. This led to a series of discussions between Beveridge, Keynes, Robbins and Epps. By 19 August Beveridge conceded the argument on pensions and thereby introduced a fundamental modification to his scheme. In a paper entitled 'The problem of pensions' Beveridge moved from a target of adequate pensions from the start to making this an ultimate goal to be achieved over a sixteen-year period. Some time after the report's publication Beveridge convinced himself that this major modification was something which he 'wanted to do in any case', recalling, 'it seemed to me right to make pensions as of right, like all other benefits in the scheme, genuinely contributory.'[23]

The other fundamental change which Beveridge made prior to publication concerned the support for children through family allowances. José Harris, in her impressive biography, describes this change as a means of concentrating resources on those in greatest need rather than one primarily aimed at limiting costs. And although it was true that the changes in family allowances limited the immediate cost to an increase of £100 millions, Harris's assertion is hardly borne out by the facts.

Originally, Beveridge envisaged a family allowance payment of five shillings per child, although, as is usual, the Cabinet papers talk of this sum as being 'illustrative' only.[24] The scheme envisaged a payment to every child including the first. But in his report Beveridge observes that a careful analysis of the studies of working-class incomes during the inter-war period showed that even the poorest wage-earners had an income to support a family with one child.

In fact, the evidence of these studies proves nothing of the kind. For example, the research findings on poverty in Sheffield,[25] Manchester[26] and Plymouth[27] are presented in such a way that it is impossible to examine the adequacy or otherwise of the main wage of the family in preventing poverty. Where enough detail does exist, such as in the Bristol study, the results show that over 40 per cent of poor households have three or fewer persons[28] and that only a minority of these can be accounted for by the inclusion of poverty among the elderly.[29]

Moreover, the studies conducted during the early years of the 1930s found, not surprisingly, that the most important cause of family poverty was unemployment. But as Britain slowly pulled out of the inter-war recession, low wages again became the key cause of poverty among families with children. As Rowntree showed in 1936, 42·3 per cent of the survey were in poverty due to an inadequate wage of the chief wage-earner. The next most important cause of poverty was unemployment of the chief wage-earner which accounted for 28·6 per cent of those who were defined as living in poverty. Old age recruited 14·7 per cent to the ranks of the poor while the death of the chief wage-earner a further 7·8 per cent.[30] Thus the major reason for limiting the scope of family allowances had little to do with the supposed findings of the inter-war poverty studies, but a great deal to do with the financial restraints imposed on Beveridge in the latter stages of preparing his report.

As a result of Beveridge's reconsideration of the scope for the provision for children, the final report contained a proposal that family allowances should not be paid to the first child in a family, and the new suggested rate only looked more generous than the original proposal until war-time inflation was taken into account. Beveridge calculated that the subsistence allowance at 1938 prices was around seven shillings a week instead of the five shillings which had been the usual figure referred to in pre-war discussions on the cost of children.[31] After allowing for wartime inflation, on the one hand, and taking account of the provision being made for children through school meals and supply of free and cheap milk on the other, Beveridge put the average allowance at eight shillings per week per child. But 'It does not follow that a cash allowance on this scale should be paid in respect to every child.' Indeed, Beveridge suggested that there were two reasons why an allowance at this level should not be paid. First, the allowances should be regarded only as a help to parents 'and not as relieving them entirely of financial responsibility'. Second, 'whatever experts may say, every mother of six knows that six children do not cost six times as much as one child to feed, clothe and keep warm.'[32] To this list Beveridge should have suggested a third reason, namely, the need to limit the scheme financially.

Government cuts

At first the government hoped it would be able to publish the Beveridge Report without attracting widespread publicity. In this they underestimated both Beveridge's determination to 'sell' his proposals and the abilities of Lord Longford (then Frank Pakenham) who helped present the plan to the media.[33] The themes that the government was dragging its feet, and that promises made in the war would be worthless after the last battle had been fought, were constantly heard, not only in the parliamentary debates in February 1943 on the Beveridge Report, but in much of the press comments which followed its publication.

'If you go below my limit you will not abolish want' was the quotation from Beveridge which the *Yorkshire Post* took as a headline announcing the report's publication in 1942. We have already seen that the plan as envisaged by Beveridge would have failed in this respect, but if we are fully to understand why the numbers in poverty have grown in the post-war world we now need also to consider the three important occasions when the government of the day reacted to the Beveridge scheme to see how further changes were made to it.

The government first replied in detail to the Beveridge plan in a parliamentary debate of February 1943. It was during this debate that the Coalition administration announced three major amendments which flawed the Beveridge plan still further. In replying to the debate, the then Home Secretary, Herbert Morrison, announced that the government rejected the idea of paying benefits generous enough to guarantee a subsistence-level income, while adding that the aim was 'to fix a benefit for unemployment and ill health on the same basis as nearly as possible'.[34] Turning to the question of pensions, Morrison cleverly presented the government's climb-down as an improvement on what Beveridge was proposing. The plan advocated a phasing-in of subsistence pensions with full pensions being paid in 1956. Morrison reported that 'the government ... may ... be able to better the Beveridge proposals at the beginning.'[35] Pensions were to be paid at a higher level at the introduction of the scheme than was advocated by Beveridge 'even if we had to make an adjustment the other way at the end'.[36]

The third major modification of the scheme centred on the provision of family allowances. We have already seen how Beveridge modified his proposals before publication in order to limit the cost of introducing the scheme. A universal benefit of five shillings per child was replaced by an allowance of eight shillings for all children except the first child of a family. The government's immediate response was to reduce this sum to five shillings a week for each eligible child. They defended this on the grounds that with the smaller benefit would come 'the development of a charter of child welfare plus ... [the] maternity and child welfare scheme ... and the development of the educational services: of school meals together with the elimination of the test for necessity.'[37] But the *quid pro quo* was never met; charges for school dinners continued, poor families receiving free dinners for their children, only after a test of means.

The White Paper chase[38]

After the parliamentary debate the Beveridge plan was committed to detailed scrutiny by Whitehall, the end result of which was the publication of two key White Papers. Commenting on their contents, Arthur Marwick records that they 'followed Beveridge remarkably closely', and he went on to observe that 'the fundamental purpose remained: a unified national insurance scheme (based on Beveridge's principles of flat-rate contributions and flat-rate benefits) which every adult member of the community must join.'[39] Similarly, Lord Bullock in his partially completed, monumental study on Ernest Bevin maintains that in the two White Papers on the report, Beveridge's proposals 'emerged unscathed and in certain respects strengthened. This was particularly true of the second White Paper which went further than Beveridge in sweeping away the old workman's compensation and proposing a national scheme for insurance against industrial injuries.'[40] While accepting Bullock's claim on the scheme for workmen's compensation, are he and Marwick right to assert that the Beveridge proposals emerged unscathed, let alone strengthened, in the government's White Papers published in 1944?

A perusal of the White Paper suggests otherwise. The three major modifications to the scheme which the government announced in early 1943 were reaffirmed in the White Papers. In the initial parliamentary debate on the scheme the government expressed a preliminary view that it would not be 'practicable' to pay benefits generous enough to prevent want or, as we would say today, poverty, and the White Paper concluded that 'further examination of the question has confirmed this view'. The White Paper observed that benefits must be paid for, and a high level of benefits would mean a high level of contribution. 'The government therefore concluded that the right objective is a rate of benefit which provides a reasonable insurance against want', in other words, at a level which, given people's savings and the like, would prevent mass claimants from becoming poor.[41]

The government defended the payment of family allowances at five shillings for second and subsequent children on the ground that the benefit 'is not intended to provide full maintenance for each child'. But the smaller benefit was to be backed by the provision of free school meals and milk to all children, the cost of which would amount to three-fifths of the cost of paying family allowances to all children. The government also confirmed the rejection of phasing in old age pensions, arguing, 'it is preferable that the new standard rate of pension, at whatever rate it may be fixed, should be payable at the time the new scheme comes into effect.'[42] While this decision was to the advantage of pensioners then, it has since resulted in condemning this group to inadequate old age pensions.

In addition the White Papers contained two further major modifications to the Beveridge scheme. One of the principles underlying the Beveridge Report was the right to draw benefits so long as need lasted. In respect to unemployment benefit, Beveridge recommended that 'Any person exhausting his claim ... will be able to continue to draw unemployment benefit without means test, subject to attendance, as required, at a work or training centre.'[43] Moreover, Beveridge realized that prolonged periods of unemployment and disability had two consequences for most claimants. In the first place the claimant's income-needs 'tend to increase rather than decrease'; secondly, measures 'other than the provision of income become increasingly necessary, to prevent deterioration in morale and to encourage recovery.'[44] To the argument that benefit must be paid as long as need lasts if poverty is to be prevented the government replied that it would be 'prudent' to limit both sickness and unemployment benefit; however the White Paper failed to mention to whom the prudence was supposed to apply.[45]

The White Paper also made major changes to the provision for women claimants. We have already seen how Beveridge himself severely curtailed the rights of women in the social security scheme. Even so, the report had recommended a marriage allowance and, more importantly, a separation allowance. The government rejected the first proposal on grounds of cost, and the second on grounds of morals. The cost of underwriting a marriage allowance was such that 'the government do not consider the benefit attractive enough to justify ... [the] charge.' On the separation allowance the government willingly allowed itself to get bogged down on the question of blame. 'The government feel that the question whether loss of maintenance is the fault of the wife is not one which should be determined by a department responsible for administering the social insurance scheme. The wife must seek other remedies open to her to secure maintenance.'[46]

One good proposal which did emerge from the White Papers was to pay a higher relative benefit for sickness and unemployment – even if for a limited duration. For a single person the proposal was to pay a retirement and invalidity benefit of twenty shillings and an unemployment and sick benefit of twenty-four shillings. For married couples the rates were thirty-five shillings and forty shillings respectively.[47]

Yet more cuts

The final major modifications to the Beveridge proposals occurred at the introduction of the scheme. In introducing the National Insurance Bill the Minister for National

Insurance confirmed the government's rejection of subsistence-level benefits. However, it was accepted that the initial level of benefits should be revised in line with rising prices. Beveridge had estimated that prices would rise by 25 per cent during the war years while the government believed it would be able to hold the rise in the cost of living to 31 per cent above the pre-war level. However, as one of the first critics of the post-war welfare state has observed, prices had already risen by far more than 31 per cent, the general price level throughout 1946 being at least 54 per cent above the pre-war level.

Moveover, the government was using the old, discredited working-class cost-of-living index to calculate the level of benefits and pensions. This index was originally drawn up in 1914 and included items like calico and candles on which working-class families spent little or no income at all. On the other hand it excluded most of the goods on which people did spend their money, apart from a small range of basic necessities. Since the prices of these basic necessities had been deliberately subsidized during the war, while other prices were allowed to rise, the index was constructed so as not to measure the real rate of inflation. Indeed, by 1946 its inadequacy was officially accepted and in the following year the new cost-of-living index took its place. Nevertheless, the old index was used to update the level of pensions which came into force in 1948.[48]

The second change which occurred at this stage was on the relative value of allowances paid to children. In calculating the needs of children, Rowntree made the arbitrary assumption that the needs of children (and women) were less than those of the adult male. This judgement, which Rowntree made at the turn of the century, went largely unquestioned in his later work, and indeed in the detailed calculations which Beveridge undertook for his report. In *Social Insurance and Allied Services* Beveridge advocated a flat-rate benefit for children which would be paid to parents drawing the main national insurance benefit as well as to those in work. Earlier in this chapter we saw how the Coalition government devalued the family allowance rate. Further modifications were made to the children's rates when the Attlee government came to determine the new national assistance rates. A child had to be aged over sixteen for the benefit payable to be greater than the rate advocated by Beveridge after the Treasury had persuaded him to modify the scope of his scheme, including the rates paid to children.

Conclusion

In this chapter we have seen that even had the scheme been implemented fully it would not have abolished poverty in the post-war world. In the first place, Beveridge underestimated the extent of family poverty which was caused by low wages. Second, the plan did not advocate a comprehensive insurance policy for women or the disabled. Third, the subsistence principle was undermined by Beveridge's unwillingness either to set benefits high enough to cover all rent levels or to adapt individual benefits to the level of rent which was actually paid.

Under Treasury pressure Beveridge then modified his proposals still further in an attempt to limit their cost. Adequate old age pensions would not be paid until 1956 and the family allowance scheme was cut back to cover only second and subsequent children in the family. Once published, the government itself announced further changes to the scheme. If a social insurance scheme was to prevent poverty, adequate benefits must be paid for as long as the claimant was without income. The government vetoed this proposal in respect to unemployment and sickness benefit. Only widows were given comprehensive coverage, leaving separated and single-parent families outside the scope of the scheme.

The scheme was modified yet again as it was about to be implemented. The concept of subsistence was abandoned, and a notional rent element was included in the calculation of flat rate benefits. Moreover, benefit levels were not revised to reflect accurately the increase in the cost of living during the war years or up to 1948 and the children's rates in the national assistance scheme were revised downwards. Two further changes were made after the introduction of the scheme. The relative level of sickness and unemployment benefit was altered and, as we shall see in the next chapter, Beveridge's proposals for the tripartite financing of the scheme were quickly torpedoed.

v. foundations
min of welfare
state insecure

5. Who Pays? – National Insurance Fund

In the third chapter we looked at the failure of the traditional welfare state to eradicate poverty. In the fourth we examined the Beveridge scheme – its conceptual faults and the fundamental modifications made during its progress towards legislation. Each modification of the Beveridge scheme helps explain some of the extent and variety of poverty today. The scheme also laid down that the traditional welfare state should have a large progressive element built into its financing. In this chapter we begin by looking at how Beveridge's financial plan was destroyed and then go on to analyse the overall impact on income distribution of financing the major part of the traditional welfare state from contributions. As part of the welfare state is financed from an Exchequer contribution, the next chapter is devoted to an analysis of the changing burden of taxation.

A contributory scheme

During the post-war period the percentage of total government expenditure devoted to social security payments rose from 13·5 per cent in 1949 to 21 per cent in 1978. A similar increase is shown if we measure social security expenditure as a percentage of gross national produce (GNP). Measured this way, social security benefits accounted for a little over 5·3 per cent of GNP in 1949, falling to 4·9 per cent two years later. From then onwards the figures show an almost continual increase until social security payments amount to almost 10·5 per cent of GNP. Whether social security payments are measured as a percentage of government expenditure or of the GNP, the picture is the same. Since the war social security payments have become bigger and bigger business and the DHSS is now the largest spending department in the government hierarchy.

The DHSS's income maintenance budget is financed from two sources – from what is called the National Insurance Fund and from general taxation. The National Insurance Fund has three sources of finance: contributions from each employed or self-employed person; contributions from the employer; and an Exchequer contribution. Over the years the National Insurance Fund has covered an increasing proportion of the rising expenditure on social security benefits. In 1945, 63 per cent of all social security benefits were paid for from the National Insurance Fund and by 1978 this had risen to 73 per cent. Over the same period of time the percentage of the social security budget being paid out of non-contributory benefits (i.e. benefits not covered by the National Insurance Fund) fell from 36 per cent to 26 per cent.

The picture remains much the same if we take out the Exchequer contribution to the National Insurance Fund and add it to the cost of all other social security payments which are covered from Exchequer payments – i.e. from taxation – and not the Insurance Fund. In 1949, 61 per cent of expenditure on social security benefits was paid for from taxation. By 1978 this had fallen to 39·5 per cent. So on both counts we see the growing importance of the contributory element of the National Insurance Fund as the means of financing the traditional welfare state. We therefore need to look carefully at how the revenue is raised to cover these payments. What are the sources of the revenue and what is the distributional impact on the individual contributor?

Writing in *Social Insurance and Allied Services*, Beveridge made a clear distinction between taxation and insurance contributions. He expressed the differences in the following terms: 'taxation is or should be related to assumed capacity to pay rather than the value of what the payer may expect to receive, while insurance contributions are or should be related to the value of the benefit and not the capacity to pay.' Moreover, Beveridge went on to say, 'whatever monies are obtained ... from insured persons as contributions and from their employers as employers, it is certain that the Exchequer, that is to say the citizen as taxpayer, must continue to meet a substantial part of the total expenditure' on the welfare state.[1] Has this been borne out in practice?

Although *Social Insurance and Allied Services* contained information on the changing proportion of the Exchequer contribution to the Fund, there is no clear description of the taxpayers' contribution to the financing of insurance benefits. For this we have to turn to the White Paper on *Social Insurance* published in 1944.[2] Here is detailed an Exchequer contribution rising from 54·1 per cent in 1945 to 59·6 per cent ten years later, rising further to 63·6 per cent in 1965, reaching 67 per cent by 1975. But as we can see from Table 7, the Exchequer contribution has nowhere

Table 7   *1944 White Paper projections – percentage shares*

	1945	1955	1965	1975
Employers/employees	43·5	38·3	34·5	31·2
Interest	2·3	2·05	1·9	1·8
Exchequer	54·1	59·6	63·6	67·02

reached these proportions. In 1955 it stood at a fraction over 13 per cent for the National Insurance Fund, rising to 15·5 per cent in 1965 and falling back to 15 per cent in 1975.

Beveridge was clear in his mind that national insurance contributions should be related to the value of the benefits which claimants would receive rather than the capacity of the contributions to pay. Obviously this places a limit on the value of benefits which could be paid as some workers' wages would be so low that they would be unable to finance more generous benefits when they were not working. However, he was also insistent that a *growing* proportion of the Fund should be financed from progressive taxation (i.e. richer groups paying a higher percentage of their income in tax) although this has not in fact happened. In the next chapter we examine how the progressiveness of the tax system has itself been eroded. Here we need to look at the two moves which governments made and which reduced drastically the progressive element in the National Insurance Fund.[3]

Vetoing the progressive element

The first move was a simple one and followed the decision to make flat-rate contributions bear an increasing proportion of the total cost of the scheme. In 1948/9, for each £3 from flat-rate contributions the government contributed £1 – itself a significant move away from the original tripartite financing advocated by Beveridge. By 1953 the government's contribution had fallen to 11·7 per cent of the National Insurance Fund, rising to 17·9 per cent by 1959 and reaching a peak of 18·1 per cent in 1961. That year saw the second major change in the financing of the Insurance Fund with the introduction of graduated contributions which were not backed by any funding from the Exchequer. Consequently, by 1978, the Exchequer contribution to the National Insurance Fund had fallen back to 14·6 per cent.

The second way by which the government cut the progressive element in the financing of the welfare state was to place an increasing reliance on graduated contributions. With little opposition the Conservative government in 1961 introduced a graduated pension scheme. Workers earning between £9 and £15 a week were required to pay a graduated contribution as well as the 'flat-rate stamp'. But as we have just noted, whereas the government made a contribution to the Exchequer to match the flat-rate contributions of work people and employers (although as we have seen they did so on a sliding scale over the years), they made no such contribution to monies arising from the graduated contributions.[4] Once introduced, graduated contributions were called upon to play an increasing role in the financing of the welfare state and by 1973/4 the total sum raised from this source was greater than the flat-rate contribution. However, it would be wrong to think that the introduction of an increased reliance on graduated contributions resulted in shifting the cost of the traditional welfare state on to those with the broadest backs. To see how successful the government was in preventing this from happening we need to examine the size of national insurance contributions which workers on different levels of income have been required to pay since the Second World War.

The individual worker's share

At the end of the inter-war period national insurance contributions represented less than 3 per cent of the adult man's industrial wage.[5] The Beveridge reforms, which came into operation in 1948, lifted this contribution to about 3·5 per cent of average earnings and in the early post-war period the trade union movement was more concerned with the failure to implement fully the Beveridge proposals than with the regressive nature of the national insurance contributions, i.e. poorer groups pay a larger percentage of their income than do other groups. In the early 1950s the unions 'offered' an increase in contributions 'if a sufficient increase in benefit could not be secured by restoring the Exchequer grant and by dipping into reserves.'[6] However, by 1954, trades union leaders were drawing attention to the increasing burden placed on lower paid workers by the national insurance stamp as it was then called. Although the TUC admitted that national insurance contributions now represented '*on average* a smaller percentage of wages than they did when the scheme was introduced ... it is, however, important to stress that average wages conceal wide variations below the average, and the above statement is not necessarily true for lower paid workers.'[7]

By 1958 national insurance contributions amounted to 3·8 per cent of average male earnings. This upward trend continued when the national insurance poll tax was modified in 1961. In that year the government introduced its earnings-related pension scheme for which, as we have just seen, contributions related to wages over the income span of £9 and £15 a week were paid in addition to the flat-rate contribution. Those earning more than £15 still paid the same graduated contributions irrespective of their income. This 'stop', or what is more usually called the 'ceiling' in the national insurance scheme, has been responsible for ensuring that the national insurance contribution became a regressive tax, particularly for male workers.

The changing incidence of national insurance contributions was noted by Dudley Jackson and his colleagues in a study on trade union wage claims and increases in real earnings. Looking at the period from 1960 to 1970 they showed the top 10 per cent of male workers contributing 2·5 per cent of their income to the National Insurance Fund at the start of the decade and 4·4 per cent of earnings at the end of the 1960s. In contrast, the bottom 10 per cent, which lost 5·4 per cent of their pay packets to the National Insurance Fund in the early sixties, were contributing 7·2 per cent to the Fund by 1970. This led the authors to observe: 'the high flat-rate element combines with the earnings' ceiling to ensure that the percentage of income taken by the contribution continues [to be] smaller as one moves up the earnings range. The new scheme did, however, make the contribution system a little less regressive at the middling or moderately high level of wages ... but this effect disappears as one moves out of the wage-incomes' normal range.'[8]

The analysis by Jackson and his colleagues covered the period up to 1970. In the years following, Sir Keith Joseph piloted on to the Statute Book a bill which made a major change to the contributory basis of the National Insurance Fund – again without a great deal of opposition. The measure, which came into force in 1975, abolished the national insurance stamp and earnings-related contributions and substituted in effect a social security tax of 5·5 per cent of earnings (since increased to 6·75 per cent in 1980/1). Moreover, the ceiling was maintained into the new scheme and the social security levy was applied to earnings between £11 and £69 a week. The floor has since been raised to £23 and the ceiling raised to £165 a week.

Once again it is this ceiling on the proportional social security tax which continues to ensure that the financing of the traditional welfare state remains regressive for male workers. At the beginning of the 1970s women at the bottom 10 per cent of earnings paid 7·8 per cent of their wages to the National Insurance Fund whereas women on three-times median earnings paid only 3·2 per cent. By 1975 the proportions had changed to 5·6 per cent and 3·7 per cent respectively. By 1979, the lowest 10 per cent of women, those earning median earnings and the top 10 per cent, all paid 6·5 per cent of their pay to the National Insurance Fund. Only beyond the top 10 per cent does the tax become more regressive and workers on three-times median earnings lose 5 per cent of their pay in national insurance contributions.

The picture is somewhat different for male workers who

make up 72 per cent of the full-time workforce. The extreme regressiveness of national insurance contributions has been somewhat abated, although there is still a marked difference between the contributions made by most workers and those on high earnings. In 1971, the poorest workers (the bottom 10 per cent) contributed 6·9 per cent of their earnings in national insurance contributions compared with 3·5 per cent contributed by those in the top 10 per cent and only 1·9 per cent by those on three-times median earnings. By 1975, the poorest workers' contribution had fallen to 5·5 per cent of earnings, the same percentage contribution as those on median earnings. Workers on the highest decile contributed a smaller percentage, 5·2 per cent, while workers on three-times median earnings still contributed only 2·3 per cent.

Since 1975 the changes in the Fund have worked against low- and high-paid workers alike. In 1979 the percentage of pay lost by the social security tax rose to 6·5 per cent of earnings for the poorest workers while workers on three-times median earnings saw their contributions raised, but only to 3·1 per cent. Workers in the top 10 per cent, paying 6 per cent of their pay to the National Insurance Fund, were still contributing less than workers on median earnings and those at the bottom.

Conclusion

The financing of the Beveridge scheme was undermined almost from the start when the government reduced the Exchequer contribution to below that envisaged in the original plan, a level which fell even lower in the following decade. In 1961 a further major change was introduced. Earnings-related pensions were financed by earnings-related contributions which themselves attracted no Exchequer supplement. Increasingly, therefore, the progressive element in the financing of the traditional welfare state has been reduced. Moreover, the size of the national insurance poll tax on employees has steadily risen since the war. In 1948 contributions stood at around 3·5 per cent of average earnings. By 1975 the poll tax was levied at 5·5 per cent. Currently, the rate has been pushed up to 6·75 per cent on earnings between £23 and £165 a week. To a significant extent, therefore, the traditional welfare state has been paid for *by working people themselves* and the contribution element has not been made an agent of re-distribution of wealth.

Although the cost of the scheme has been progressively shifted on to workers and their employers the Exchequer contributed over £1·5 billion in 1978 to the National Insurance Fund. In addition, taxation paid for the whole range of non-contributory benefits, such as supplementary benefits. In order to complete the analysis of who pays for the welfare state we need to look at the British tax system. In the following chapter we examine the changing tax base from which monies are raised to cover part of the cost of the welfare state. In doing so we will see how the British tax system has moved from a progressive to a proportional system of taxation. This change has come about largely due to the rise of three of the other four welfare states which we will consider further in Chapters 7 to 10.

6. Who Pays? – Taxation

There are two reasons why it is important to look at the shifts in taxation. First, towards the end of the 1970s almost 40 per cent of the social security budget was paid for from the Exchequer, and it is crucial to see who shoulders this burden. Second, the tax system lays the basis for the other four welfare states with which we are concerned. This chapter will therefore be about the three important shifts in the incidence of tax during the post-war period: a vertical shift of direct taxation from the rich to the poor, and a horizontal shift from single people and childless couples on to taxpayers with children, as well as a more recent movement from direct to indirect taxation. It is also concerned with the share of income paid in tax by different groups. For this we shall draw on some of the information on the distribution of income presented in Chapter 1 to examine the extent to which changes in the burden of taxation can be explained by changes in the share of gross income going to different income groups. Finally, it will examine the extent to which it is tenable, given the inadequacy of the relevant data, to argue that inequalities in the tax system are mitigated once the benefits of the welfare state are taken into account.

Changing pattern of taxation

The rate and distribution of taxation generates and sustains many myths. One is that direct taxation makes up an increasing proportion of government revenue. This is not true. The percentage of total government revenue raised from direct taxation rose from 29·1 per cent in 1946 to 37·3 per cent in 1976. Since then there has been a sharp decline in the proportion of total revenue raised from taxes on personal income, and in 1979 only 29·6 per cent of central government revenue came from this source. The proportion of revenue derived from expenditure taxes has similarly changed. In 1946 36·1 per cent of central government finance came from indirect taxation. This proportion fell over the years reaching a low ebb of 26·4 per cent in 1975. Since then each year has seen an increase and by 1979 expenditure taxes raised 35·1 per cent of all central government finance.

Two other major changes occurred over this period. First, the years since 1946 show a marked increase in the proportion of central government revenue being raised by way of social security contributions. In 1946 the employees' contribution amounted to 2·4 per cent of the total tax take. By 1979 this had risen to 6·9 per cent. The increase in employers' social security contribution is even more marked; up from 2·3 per cent in 1946 to 10·2 per cent in 1979. Second, in a period when the size of the government's budget increased in real terms it is not surprising to find a real increase in the rates of taxation. The one exception to this general trend concerns company taxation. In 1946, taxes levied on companies amounted to 18·4 per cent of total government revenue. By 1979 this had fallen to 7·4 per cent.

A number of trends are therefore clear. The contribution to the National Insurance Fund from employers and employees has grown significantly in the post-war period. The proportions of total government revenue being raised from direct and indirect taxation shows an important shift to indirect taxation over the past few years and this is a trend accentuated by the Conservative government elected in 1979. Given that expenditure taxes now amount to 35 per cent of the total tax take, it is necessary to look in a little more detail at the distributional impact of recent indirect tax changes.

(i) Indirect taxation

Central government taxes on expenditure consist of excise duties on home-produced goods and services as well as on goods imported from abroad, the value added tax (VAT) and car tax, protective import duties together with stamp duties and other miscellaneous taxes on expenditure. The most important of these taxes in terms of revenue are excise duties and VAT, and it is possible to argue, as some government spokesmen recently have, that VAT is not regressive. In his 1979 Budget the Chancellor did just that. After reminding the House that large areas of consumer spending are not chargeable to VAT, Sir Geoffrey Howe went on to argue that as poorer households spend proportionately more of their income on such zero-rated goods, 'VAT is not regressive.'[1] However, to argue this way, it is necessary to calculate the effects of VAT on expenditure rather than on disposable income. Once a person's disposable income is taken as the base line the regressiveness of indirect tax becomes more apparent. For example, in 1977 the 2·5 per cent of the top 10 per cent's income went in VAT. This contrasts with 3·3 and 3·1 per cent of the incomes of the ninth and tenth decile respectively.

Because of the regressiveness of indirect taxation disquiet was expressed by the poverty lobby at the Conservative government's proposal to switch the balance of taxation from direct to indirect in the 1979 Budget. More significantly, caution on the proposed switch to VAT was also advocated by the civil service, and a confidential minute prepared by the DHSS was passed to the *New Statesman*. According to the *New Statesman* this minute stated: 'It is clear that a shift from income tax to commodity taxation would help the rich and hurt the poor.' The minute then went on to explain the distributional impact on the poor of increasing the percentage of total government revenue coming from indirect taxation.

The poorest 10 per cent of households pay, at present, considerably more tax on their expenditure than on their income and this is true even if subsidies are taken into account. This occurs even though on average the commodity tax payment by households is lower than the income tax payment and occurs because the income tax system through its allocation of tax-free allowances prevents the very poor from paying tax. In contrast, the income tax payment of the richest 20 per cent of households is nearly double their commodity tax payment ... over 10 per cent of the commodity tax burden before subsidies is borne by the poorest 20 per cent of households compared with only 3·8 per cent of the income tax burden and 4·7 per cent of national insurance contributions.

The minute went on to argue:

An additional £1 in tax has a greater effect on a pensioner earning only £30 a week than it does on a millionaire. So to measure the progressivity or otherwise of a system of taxation it is useful to compare the tax payment of each household with its disposable income. The tax could be said to be progressive if the proportion of disposable income of the poorer households which is paid in tax is lower than that of richer households. On this measure commodity taxation as it existed in 1977 was regressive.

Patrick Wintour, commenting on the minute, emphasized that the poorest 10 per cent paid 19 per cent of their disposable income in commodity tax while the richest 20 per cent paid only 15 per cent. But it is important to remember that these calculations have been made after adding back the effect of rent and rate rebates. Even so, indirect taxation is shown to be regressive. The minute concluded with the following observation: 'It is the pensioners and one-parent families, many of whom pay no income tax, but who do purchase taxed goods who would lose most.'[2] It would have been truer to have said that all low income groups would be similarly affected.

Low-income groups were affected most by the switch from direct to indirect taxation in the 1979 Budget. The Chancellor increased the standard rate of VAT from 8 per cent to 15 per cent and the luxury rate of VAT from 12·5 per cent to 15 per cent. This gave a further twist to the regressiveness of indirect taxation. Those on incomes of £3000 a year saw a 3-percentage-points increase in the amount of income paid in indirect taxation compared to only 1·6 percentage points for those on £15,000 a year and a mere 0·87 per cent for those on incomes of £30,000.

(ii) Direct taxation

As we have seen, there has been an important shift in the burden of taxation in the post-war years from companies on to individuals. Part of this shift has been also brought about by the increase in the revenue raised from expenditure taxes. We now turn and examine what has happened in the post-war years to the burden of direct taxation, and here two trends are discernible. First, since the war, the number of taxpayers has grown: up from 13·5 million in 1945 to over 21 million today. This increase is way in excess of any growth of the working population and highlights the extent to which poorer people have been brought into tax. If working wives are counted separately, the number of individual taxpayers stood at around 25·6 million in 1979/80. Second, the burden of tax has increased most for the poor and for taxpayers with children, almost irrespective of how rich or poor they are.

The normal way of examining the changing burden of income tax is to relate the tax threshold (the point at which one begins to pay tax) to a measuring rod which in most tax debates is average earnings. An examination of the tax threshold for different tax-paying units – the single person, married couple, married couple with different numbers of children – gives us the following picture. In 1949/50, while a single person began to pay tax at a fraction below 40 per cent of average earnings (now 24·7 per cent), a married couple with one wage packet did not contribute a penny in direct taxation until they earned almost 63 per cent of average earnings (now 38·5 per cent). A two-wage-earning married couple without children paid their first income tax when their earnings were equal to the average wage packet (now 63.2 per cent). In the same year, a married couple with two children but only one wage earner, began paying income tax at a fraction below average earnings (now 43·5 per cent). A family with four children were exempt from tax until their income was more than 130 per cent of average earnings (now it is 47·7 per cent).

So while it is true to say that the tax threshold has fallen for every type of income taxpayer, it has not fallen equally fast for all groups. Over the period from 1949/50 the tax threshold has *fallen* by 37·3 per cent for a single person, 38·6 per cent for a married couple and by 36·8 per cent for a two-wage-earning married couple. Much more significant reductions are recorded for households with children. For a married couple with one child under eleven, the tax threshold fell during the period from 1949/50 by 50·4 per cent. For a married couple with two children the fall was 56·4 per cent. The larger the family, the more significant was the fall in the tax threshold measured as a percentage of average earnings. A family with three children saw a reduction in the tax threshold of 60·2 per cent, and for a four-child family the reduction was 76·9 per cent.

Another way of measuring the changes in the tax threshold for different types of taxpayers is to present the threshold as an index figure rather than as a percentage of average earnings, with 1948/9 equalling 100. Such an analysis shows that while the tax threshold in money terms (as opposed to real terms) has increased for all taxpayers, it has increased fastest for married couples without children and for single people. While families with four children have seen their tax threshold in money terms rise from 100 to 498, the tax threshold for a single person has risen from 100 in 1948/9 to 809 in 1979/80.

This information on changes in the tax threshold shows two important shifts in the tax burden in the post-war period. Over the years, people on lower and lower incomes have been called upon to pay tax. But this vertical shift in the burden of taxation has not been shared equally; over the post-war period the burden of tax has increased faster for taxpayers responsible for children, i.e. a horizontal shift. The combined effect of both the vertical and horizontal shift in the tax burden can be seen again from Table 8. This starts with the tax burden for different groups in 1949 and measures the percentage increase in tax and national insurance contributions over the post-war

Table 8 *Percentage changes in the amount of income paid in tax and national insurance, 1949/50 to 1978/9 (and data to 1979/80)*

Earnings level	Single person	Married couple	Married couple + two children	Married couple + four children
2/3rds average	54·3	71·4	70·5	65·9
	(52·1)	(70·3)	(71·9)	(72·2)
average	49·0	61·5	85·8	84·8
	(45·9)	(60·7)	(85·6)	(85·4)
2 × average	25·8	34·3	54·4	69·8
	(19·3)	(28·8)	(51·2)	(68·5)
5 × average	37·9	38·9	43·5	47·6
	(24·1)	(25·5)	(31·9)	(37·8)
10 × average	33·4	33·8	35·1	36·7
	(12·9)	(15·2)	(15·5)	(17·6)

Source: reworked figures from *Hansard*, Vol. 979, Cols. 174–8, 19 February 1980.

period. The main body of the table details the percentage changes in income paid in tax and national insurance over the period 1949/50 to 1978/9. The figures in brackets take into account the major tax changes brought about by the Thatcher administration's first budget.

By and large it is those on average and two-thirds average earnings who have seen the greatest percentage increase in their income being taken in tax and national insurance deductions. Over the period up to 1978/9 the share of contributions to the Exchequer for a single person on two-thirds average earnings increased by 54·3 per cent. For a married couple the increase was in the order of 71·4 per cent, falling to 70·5 per cent for a married couple on two-thirds average earnings with two children, and to 65·9 per cent for a married couple with four children. A similar slight fall is recorded in the share of income paid in tax for a family on average earnings.

For all other groups in the table the percentage share of income paid in tax rises for taxpayers with children. For example, a single taxpayer on average earnings saw a 49 per cent increase in his tax bills during the period up to 1978/9 whereas the increase was in the order of 84·8 per cent for a taxpayer on average earnings with four children. This trend is even more marked for a taxpayer on twice average earnings. A single person's tax bill increased by 25·8 per cent whereas the same taxpayer on twice average earnings saw his tax bill increased by 69·8 per cent if he had four children. An increasing tax burden correlated with family size can also be seen for taxpayers on five and ten times average earnings, although the differences are far less significant.

In 1979 the incoming Conservative government reduced taxation by a little over £4·5 billion. Of this, the richest 7 per cent of taxpayers gained 34 per cent of all the tax cuts, a total of £1560 million. The poorest 10 per cent gained only 2 per cent of the tax cuts. The effect this had on the share of incomes paid in tax and national insurance is presented in brackets in Table 8. The tax cuts have had a two-way effect. For those on average and below-average earnings the tax burden has actually increased for those with children, and this is particularly marked for those on two-thirds average earnings. And whereas the tax cuts for childless taxpayers on these levels of earnings have been almost insignificant, the changes for other taxpayers grow as income rises. The tax cuts were so large that the Thatcher government's first Budget has in all probability brought about the most significant redistribution of income in the post-war period – and this change has been wholly to the advantage of the rich. For a single person on ten times average earnings the percentage increase in taxes over this period has been cut from 33·4 per cent to 12·9 per cent. For a taxpayer with four children on ten times average earnings the reduction is in the order of 36·7 per cent down to 17·6 per cent.

This trend was continued in the 1980 Budget. The richest 2 per cent took 14 per cent of the total net tax reductions. In addition, the burden of taxation was shifted once again on to taxpayers with children. Although child benefits were increased in the Budget (up by 9·5 per cent on an annual basis), the increase was less than the changes in the personal tax allowances (up by 11 per cent).

The argument that the burden of taxation has shifted on to the poor and to families is not universally accepted. One counter-argument centres on the changing shares of income; a second, on the overall distributional impact of taxes and benefits. We look at each counter-view in turn.

Changing income shares

It is stressed in some quarters that the reason why the above analysis shows the very highest income earners experiencing smaller percentage increases in the incidence of taxation is due to the fact that their share of total income on which they pay tax has continued to fall in the post-war period; hence they have a relatively smaller income base on which to pay tax; hence the declining share of total tax take from the rich. This argument is not sustained when we examine the changing incidence of taxation on different income groups and then relate this information to changes in the distribution of pre-taxed income. The data in Table 9 illustrate the changes in the percentage of total revenue raised from each decile group over the past twenty years.

From this we can see that whereas in 1949/50 the top 10 per cent of taxpayers contributed 72 per cent of all income tax (including surtax), this proportion had fallen to 35 per cent in 1978/9. The effect of this considerable reduction has been an increase in the percentage share of tax paid for all other decile groups except the poorest 10 per cent. The richest 10 to 20 per cent of income recipients, for example, paid 9 per cent of the total amount raised in income tax in 1949/50 and 16 per cent in 1978/9.

It is important to note that over this period of time we have already recorded a considerable increase in the total sum of money raised by income tax: up from £1½ billion in 1949/50 to over £18 billion in 1976/7. Given their present share of total income, it is impossible for the richest 10 per cent of income recipients to continue to contribute 72 per cent of the £18 billions-or-so raised in income tax in 1976/7. What is important, however, is to examine changes in the share of total income tax raised from different income groups against a background of variations in the share of pre-taxed income.

Since 1949/50, total personal income rose from around £10 billion to over £90 billion. The top 10 per cent in the late 1940s gained 33 per cent of pre-taxed income and paid 72 per cent of tax revenue. By 1976/7 the top 10 per cent had 26 per cent of pre-taxed income and paid 35 per cent of tax revenue (a proportion which is still falling, for the latest figures for 1980/1 show a drop to 32·7 per cent).[3] Given that the top 10 per cent had 33 per cent of income

Table 9 *Percentage shares of tax paid by different income groups 1949/50 to 1978/9*

	Year[a]										
	1949/50	1959/60	1970/1	1971/2	1972/3	1973/4	1974/5	1975/6	1976/7	1977/8	1978/9[c]
Top 10 per cent	72	57	41	39	40	38	37	35	35	35	35
10–20 per cent	9	12	15	15	14	14	15	15	15	15	16
20–30 per cent	5	7	11	12	11	12	11	12	12	12	12
30–40 per cent	3	6	9	9	9	9	10	10	10	10	10
40–50 per cent	3	5	7	8	8	8	8	8	8	8	8
50–60 per cent	3	4	6	6	6	7	7	7	7	7	7
60–70 per cent	2	4	5	5	5	5	5	5	6	6	5
70–80 per cent	1	3	3	3	4	4	4	4	4	4	4
80–90 per cent	1	1	2	2	2	2	2	3	2	2	2
Bottom 10 per cent	1	1	1	1	1	1	1	1	1	1	1
Total tax[b] (£m)	1101	1735	5158	6356	6572	8045	11,846	15,987	18,300	18,200	20,400

a. Years up to and including 1972/3 take income tax and surtax together. Subsequent years relate to income tax (including higher rates and the additional rate on investment income).

b. Married couples are counted as one taxpayer. Only tax paid by individuals (i.e. excluding trusts etc.) is included.

c. 1978/9 is a provisional estimate.

Source: House of Lords *Hansard*, cols. 739–40, 31 January 1978, and *Hansard*, col. 365, 24 January 1980.

in the late 1940s, the same proportion in 1976/7 would have given them £30 billion instead of the £24 billion they in fact possessed. On this higher sum (£30 billion) they would have paid around £8 billion in tax rather than the £6 billion they in fact did pay. Thus, less than a third of the fall in the proportion of tax revenue paid can be accounted for by a fall of the top 10 per cent's share of income.

Consequently, the burden has risen for those lower down the income distribution who have been paying increasingly for the real growth in the expenditure on welfare. But even this analysis is said to be incomplete by some critics who argue that the overall view of redistribution in the welfare state has to include the effects on living standards of paying back benefits for which contributions are made either through the National Insurance Fund or from direct and indirect taxation. We now turn to examine this belief in more detail.

Taxes and benefits combined

Since 1962 the Central Statistical Office (CSO) has published annually an analysis of the incidence of taxes and social benefits. From this the CSO asserts that the overall effect of collecting taxes and contributions and then paying out benefits is to redistribute resources to those on low income as well as to those with children. But does a careful look at the CSO series bear out this widely held belief? In order to answer this question we need to review the work of those commentators who have suggested that such sweeping conclusions cannot be supported by the evidence presented by the CSO.

Writing in 1968, Alan Peacock and Robin Shannon argued that no reliable conclusions could be drawn on the overall effect of combining tax payments and social security benefits when the analysis was based on a little over a third of government expenditure and only a half of tax revenues.[4] The most recent analysis from the CSO for 1978 covers 59 per cent of government receipts and 46 per cent of all government expenditure.

Since 1968 a number of studies have tried to calculate the distributionary effects of including in the analysis a higher percentage of the taxes levied and the benefits distributed in the welfare state. This work shows the allocation of the missing tax revenue and social benefits as having an important impact on the level of redistribution brought about by the welfare state, and pioneering work on this front has been carried out by J. L. Nicholson. Reporting recently, Nicholson and a colleague, A. J. C. Britton, made two sets of assumptions about allocating the residual. These were that benefits of all unallocated expenditure, and the cost of unallocated taxation, fell equally on each individual, or that the net benefit from unallocated expenditure less tax fell on households in proportion to their final income. Their conclusion was that 'The extent of vertical redistribution is rather crucially dependent on the treatment of the residual.'[5]

We noted earlier that this country's poverty scales underestimate the relative costs of children. Likewise, we have seen in this chapter how the tax burden has increased fastest for households with children, and it is in this respect that the conclusion of Jane Peretz's work on the allocation of the residual tax and benefits in the CSO's studies is particularly important to an analysis of the extent to which the overall effect of taxes and benefits favours households with children.[6] Peretz also added back a large proportion of the public expenditure which is excluded from the CSO analysis. Her findings were that 'the general effect of including these additional categories has probably been to reduce somewhat the degree of redistribution to some households which is implied. This is because these categories of expenditure are mostly on services etc. used by the whole population or, in some cases, used more by the better-off.' Moreover, the 'net effect of having better information about the uses of the various services could be to make a further reduction in the degree of redistribution implied.'

This conclusion needs to be borne in mind, for the main cluster of benefits which are allocated in the CSO analysis are the payment of cash allowances and the use of the main welfare-state services such as schools and hospitals. Those benefits and services which are easiest to allocate in the analysis are predominantly used by families with children and by pensioners. Both Nicholson's and Peretz's work show that to include some of the residual lessens the redistributionary effect; Peretz also suggests that to include other forms of unallocated public expenditure will lessen still further their redistributionary gains marked up to the poor and to households with children.

The belief that the welfare state redistributes generously towards families, to such an extent as to offset the increased burden of taxation among this group, is undermined still further by the pathfinding study conducted by Muriel Nissel. In this she begins by emphasizing the relative increase in the burden of taxation for families with children, to which reference has already been made. Nissel then used the CSO data to look at the redistribution brought about by the welfare state. It is important to remember that she is using data which have not been adjusted for the large percentage of taxes and benefits which remain unallocated and which the work of Nicholson, Britton and Peretz suggests lessens what redistribution there has been to low-income groups and to families.

As well as presenting CSO data, Nissel reworks the material on the basis of adult equivalent scales, adding that these calculations are 'admittedly rough and ready but they are sufficient to bring home the point that the income available to individuals and households varies considerably at different stages of the life cycle and that it matters a great deal how many types of people live in these households.'[7]

CSO data on disposable household income after tax and

benefits for a four-child family on a household basis show this group faring in 1976 very slightly better than other groups. However, once the data are reworked on an adult equivalent basis, a four-child family is shown to be slightly worse off than the average retired couple, and having only about half as much as a non-retired couple without children. On the basis of the reworked data, Nissel concludes that 'For the average household with children ... cash benefits (including indirect benefits such as housing and food subsidies) were small and substantially outweighed by taxes.'[8]

The studies by Nicholson and Peretz point to the following conclusions. First, it is dangerous to generalize from the CSO studies about the extent of redistribution within the welfare state when such a large part of the taxes collected and benefits consumed are left out of the analysis. Second, when these unaccounted-for sums are added back, the extent to which the payment of taxes and the receipts of benefits help the poor is greatly reduced. Thirdly, Nissel's pioneering study shows that it is not possible to argue that the tax burden of families with children is offset by their being awarded a disproportionate share in what has become known as the social wage.

Conclusion

Expenditure on the traditional welfare state has risen in real terms in the post-war period and particularly since the mid-1960s. While the national insurance contributions finance a major part of the traditional welfare state, a significant sum comes from taxation. This chapter has been concerned with the changing burden of taxation in the post-war period, and particularly over the past fifteen or twenty years. We have seen, first, that there has been a marked shift in the burden of taxation from companies on to individuals. A second major change in more recent years has been an important shift to indirect taxation, with a consequential movement in the burden of taxation against those on lower incomes. Thirdly, the burden of direct taxation has changed, workers on lower and lower incomes being called upon to pay an increasing share of the tax burden, and we have seen that this change cannot be explained away by more equal redistribution of pre-tax income. A fourth major shift in the burden of taxation has been a horizontal movement from single people and child-less couples on to taxpayers with children, irrespective of their level of earnings. While these changes have been taking place steadily over the past couple of decades under governments of both parties, the Thatcher government's tax changes have brought about a similar change in the tax burden but within the space of a single budget.

This shift in the tax burden on to the poor and on to taxpayers with children has not been countered by the payment of benefits. The extent of redistribution of resources to the poor and to those with children, which is sometimes alleged to have been brought about by the total impact of the collection of taxes on one hand, and the payment of benefits on the other, has been shown to be very questionable. We now need to examine the mechanisms by which the burden of taxation has been shifted both vertically on to the poor and horizontally on to families during the post-war period when large sections of the electorate believe the opposite has occurred. In doing so, we shall begin our discussions on the other welfare states which are supported through the tax system.

7. The Tax Allowance Welfare State

The cost of the traditional welfare state has risen in real terms since the end of the Second World War and has been paid for largely by contributions weighing most heavily on poorer members of the community. Despite this, the widespread belief is that increasingly welfare has resulted in a crippling burden of taxation on the rich. The last chapter showed that there has indeed been a two-fold shift in the direct tax burden over the last twenty to thirty years; vertically on to those with lower incomes and horizontally on to those taxpayers with children. So why is the myth about the crippling burden of taxation on the rich so persistent? The apparent evidence of high taxation obscures the growth of a second welfare state, based on tax benefits which are of greatest value to those on high incomes. The tax-allowance welfare state is the subject of this chapter, which begins by examining the total income available for taxation and the amount of this income which is secured tax-free by means of the growth of the tax-allowance welfare state. The chapter then examines the range of the tax-allowance welfare state and its distributional impact at different levels of income.

Getting off tax-free

The present system of British income tax works on the basis of awarding allowances which can be set against taxable income. Income increasingly covers (although, as we shall see, not nearly adequately enough) both money income and some forms of income in kind, such as free houses and cars. Against this income a taxpayer is allowed to offset what are called his personal allowances together with other deductions which considerably reduce the cost of certain 'approved' expenditure, such as the purchasing of a house by way of a mortgage. Recently, these allowances and deductions have been described as 'tax expenditures', and they are expenditures in the sense that by the granting of each allowance or deduction, tax revenue is lost and the total tax base diminished.

It would be wrong to pretend that this way of viewing tax concessions has been universally accepted. After some reluctance, the Callaghan government published in its final White Paper on public expenditure the first official list of tax expenditures. The White Paper states that there are difficulties in defining tax expenditures and says: 'In short, this approach can be usefully related to some tax reliefs, but there is no agreement as to the criteria governing its application and the field within which it can be applied'.[1]

The idea that it is difficult for governments to estimate the losses for granting tax relief is disputed by Stanley S. Surrey, who is one of the originators of the concept of tax expenditure. Professor Surrey has written:

> While some appear to regard the task of estimation as bordering on the impossible, a moment's thought will indicate that the estimation of revenue losses for particular tax provisions is a regular task for government technicians. Each time a change in the tax law is proposed, a revenue figure must be attached to the change. The estimates may sometimes be difficult to make for lack of data, but they are made, and tax expenditure estimates are no different.[2]

Pioneering work in this country, calling for a tax expenditure budget, was undertaken by J. R. M. Willis and P. J. W. Hardwick who work at the Centre for Fiscal

Studies at the University of Bath. In their book *Tax Expenditures in the United Kingdom* the authors define a tax expenditure as 'an exemption or relief which is not part of the essential structure of the tax in question but has been introduced into the tax code for some extraneous reason – e.g. in order to ease the burden for a particular class of taxpayer, or to provide an incentive to apply income in a particular way, or perhaps to simplify administration.' The authors go on to say: 'The term is used to cover not merely specific exemptions but also gaps in the charge, as a result of which receipts or benefits which represent or are equivalent to income are not subjected to tax'. And they conclude: 'The choice of the term "tax expenditure" indicates that because they are not inherent in the structure of the tax, these reliefs are equivalent in terms of revenue foregone to direct government expenditure and should in general be judged by the same criteria.'[3]

How valid is the Willis and Hardwick distinction between tax benefits, which they describe as being essential to the structure of the tax system, and other tax benefits, which are not viewed in the same way and which are called, by them, tax expenditures? A moment's thought on this issue shows the difficulties of maintaining what I believe to be a false distinction. At one point, Willis and Hardwick defend their approach on the grounds that 'Some initial exemption is essential to the structure of a tax which bases itself on the ability to pay.'[4] They quote the findings of the 1955 Royal Commission on taxation to the effect that it is a well-established belief that income tax should not be levied on incomes which are below the poverty line. But this ignores a very crucial argument and discourages the reader from thinking about other ways by which the revenue lost in granting some of the personal tax reliefs could be used to guarantee a tax-free sum for everybody in the community, or to protect the poor from paying tax. The campaign by Lady Rhys-Williams to establish a social dividend was one which sees the abolition of the present tax-benefit system and its replacement by cash payments to everybody. In a more limited way the Heath government's Green Paper on tax credits embodied the same principles. Indeed, the tax-credits proposals were the most radical proposals for reforming the benefit and tax welfare states put forward by a government since the 1950s. The Green Paper laid down proposals for tax credits which could be set against tax liability. Those not earning, or not earning enough to offset their tax liability against the full credit, would be given a cash payment.

It is possible to take this idea a stage further and advocate the granting of personal tax allowances or tax credits which are only of value to those on low income. Indeed, this was the system which operated up until 1920. The exemption system, as its name suggests, exempted those on low incomes from paying tax but did not grant those tax concessions to people irrespective of their level of income. As we shall see in a moment, the personal allowances 'cost' the Exchequer an enormous sum each year, for the simple reason that they are granted to everybody irrespective of their level of income. In arguing that some of the personal allowances are crucial to the structure of income tax, Willis and Hardwick ignore that the same objective – namely, of exempting the poor from tax – could be achieved in other ways at far less cost. I do not believe, therefore, that their distinction between granting reliefs which are crucial to the tax structure on the one hand, and tax expenditures on the other, can or should be maintained. Thus, tax benefits are defined in this book as the granting of all those tax concessions, whether they be personal allowances, exemptions or reliefs from tax, which narrow the tax base.

The birth of modern taxation

Just before the outbreak of the First World War total government expenditure was £184 million a year. By 1916 it had risen ten-fold – to £1825 million – and this necessitated a massive increase in the rates of income tax. In order to spread this load fairly, and weight the increases towards those with fewest responsibilities, the government introduced a whole series of allowances – based on marital status and dependants – which form the basis of the present system of personal allowances.

In the 1917 Budget, the Chancellor, Bonar Law, first allowed taxpayers with incomes up to £700 to claim a child allowance for each child which, since 1915, had stood at £25 per child. In his 1918 Budget an allowance of £25 was allowed for a taxpayer's wife, and so began the married man's tax allowance. The same sum was allowed for widowers with related housekeepers and for those taxpayers with dependent relatives. The 1917 Budget also extended the tax allowance for children to those on incomes from £800 to £1000 a year and to those with three or more children.

Since 1917 there have been two major changes in the value of tax allowances. The first occurred in 1920 when the whole of the British system of direct taxation was changed from an exemption to an allowance system. Up until that point, tax allowances could be claimed but were only of value for people with income below a certain prescribed level. For example, when Lloyd George reintroduced children's allowances in 1909 they were valued at £10 and could be claimed only by taxpayers with incomes below £500 a year. In 1920, tax allowances could be claimed by any taxpayer, irrespective of their income, but only at the standard rate. This was changed in 1956/7 when the excess value of child tax allowances and other allowances for dependants over the single personal allowance became allowable at the•surtax rate. The excess value of the additional personal allowance was likewise allowed at the higher rate of tax in 1960/1.

The 1920 Budget was important in another respect. A Royal Commission, established in 1919 to enquire into all aspects of income tax, proposed a 'personal allowance', a recommendation which was implemented by Austen Chamberlain in his 1920 Budget. In one sense, therefore, the personal allowances may be said to date from 1920.

The wife's earned-income relief was also introduced in 1920 in order to give some compensation to working wives for the extra cost of going out to work. The allowance was originally set at such a level that a married couple who were both earning gained the same tax exemptions as two single people. During the Second World War the value of the wife's earned-income relief was increased dramatically in order to encourage women to become part of the war economy. The allowance was raised to equal that of the full single person's allowance but could be claimed only at the standard rate. Later, the allowance became more valuable as the working wife was also allowed to claim against her tax allowance the reduced rates of tax. A further major reform came in the 1972/3 tax year when husbands and wives were given the option of being taxed as two single persons. The wife was given her own tax rate, and in return the husband surrendered the married person's tax allowance. Further, under the unified tax system where the wife was not taxed separately from her husband, the wife's earned-income relief was set against the combined income of the couple and therefore was set against their marginal, i.e. their highest, rate of tax.

A major concession has been made to elderly taxpayers with the granting of the age allowance which stands at £1820 for a single taxpayer and £2895 for a married couple. The tax threshold for a single pensioner is therefore £445 above the threshold for a non-pensioner, and £750 above the normal threshold for a married couple who are not pensioners. This concession is limited to those on lower incomes. If the pensioner's income (or the household income if both have incomes) is above £5900, the pensioner pays a marginal tax rate of 50 per cent until the additional value of the age allowance is wiped out. This happens when the pensioner's income exceeds £6567.50 and that of a married couple exceeds £7025.

A shrinking tax base

(i) Personal tax benefits

The extent to which the personal allowances have eroded the tax base can be seen from the following information. The main personal allowances are the single person's allowance (valued currently in 1980/1 at £1375 a year), the married person's allowance (currently valued at £2145 a year), the wife's earned-income relief (also at £1375), and the additional personal allowance which stands at the same as the married man's tax relief. In addition, there are further personal allowances which include smaller allowances for housekeepers, blind persons and dependent relatives.

While one of the major reasons for granting personal allowances is to guarantee that the poorest do not pay income tax, this objective is not achieved. At the present time the tax threshold for a single person is a little below £25 a week, but the supplementary benefit poverty line is above this, standing at £28.70. Similarly, for a married couple, while the tax threshold stands at £41.25, the supplementary benefit poverty line is £42. So, despite a massive erosion of the tax base (to the tune of over £19 million) this basic objective of the tax system is not achieved.

The extent of the erosion of the tax base can be seen again by looking at the amount of income the allowances exempt from tax and measuring this against the total amount of income liable for tax in any one year. The Inland Revenue statistics for 1979 give details on the total of income liable to tax and the extent to which this total is diminished by the granting of various tax benefits.[5] In 1976/7, the Inland Revenue put total net personal income at £80,800 million. Against this sum were allowed the full range of personal allowances amounting to £30,900 million of tax-free income – accounted for in the following ways.

The income exempted by the married person's tax allowance in 1976/7 amounted to £12,600 million. The single person's allowance exempted £6700 million from tax, and the wife's earned-income relief a further £4290 million. The age allowance exempted £3260 million of pensioners' income from tax and child tax allowances a further £4160 million. In 1976/7, child tax allowances still existed, although they have now been replaced by child benefits. These allowances for children were partially offset by £285 million in clawback arrangements, while other personal tax allowances exempted £225 million from tax. Thus, only £50,000 million was liable to tax. From this the total tax raised was £18,300 million.

More comprehensive figures have been given in the latest White Paper on public expenditure, which lists well over ninety tax benefits. The main costs (or revenue lost) of the tax benefit welfare state come from the granting of personal tax reliefs (£12,930), the exemption of the first £500 of investment income from investment income surcharge (costing £780 millions), the granting of mortgage interest relief (now at a cost estimated at £1450 millions), the massive tax relief to companies (estimated in the current year to be approaching £6000 millions), stamp duty exemptions (probably costing £1300 millions in the present financial year), exempting owner-occupied houses from capital gains tax (put at a cost of £2000 millions) plus double taxation reliefs (which are well in excess of £2500 millions).[6] These tax benefits have immensely important distributional effects and we need to look at some of them in a little more detail to see when they were granted and what were the grounds for exempting income from taxation.

(ii) Housing tax benefits

Owner-occupation is supported by three tax benefits: mortgage interest relief, the exemption from capital gains tax, and the abolition of Schedule A. From the very start until 1963, tax was charged on the annual value of land and this included houses and other buildings irrespective of whether the property was let, at what level the rent was levied, or whether the property was owner-occupied. This system of taxation, which was known generally as Schedule A tax was not without its critics and the campaign against it increased momentum from 1957, when amendments were moved to the Budget statement to make exemptions or partial exemptions to Schedule A. The tax was finally abolished in 1963, one reason being, as Hardwick and Willis note, that 'In the UK the social benefits of home ownership were regarded, when it came to the point, as the overriding consideration.'[7] The abolition of Schedule A did not affect the rate of increase in the number becoming owner-occupiers, although some critics maintain that if it had not been abolished the steady rise to the current 53-per-cent owner-occupation level would have been slowed down.

It is difficult to compute the current loss in revenue (or gain to individual owner-occupiers) of Schedule A's abolition. A guesstimate can be made by revaluing the revenue from Schedule A in 1980 prices. But even here we run into difficulties. Data on the revenue gained from Schedule A are available only as far back as 1949/50. Before that they were not published by the Inland Revenue and, when these data were requested, the Revenue replied that 'the Board of Inland Revenue is unable to supply exact figures' for years prior to this date. Reworking the 1949 net revenue from Schedule A (which stood at £102 million) gives a total of £770 million in January 1980 prices. By 1951/2 the amount had fallen to £691 million in 1980 prices, by 1953/4 to £560 millions, by 1955/6 to £499 millions, rising again to over £500 millions in 1960/1. Only with the phasing out of Schedule A – from 1963/4 onwards – does the total revenue begin to fall appreciably.

A somewhat higher figure in lost revenue is given by Hardwick and Willis. They suggest that if the charge were reintroduced with the current rateable values for owner-occupied houses adopted as the measure of the notional income, 'the additional tax yield for 1974/5 would have been some £930 million'.[8] While the first calculations take no account of the real rise in imputed rent from owner-occupation, these second calculations by Hardwick and Willis are based on rateable values which are themselves now outdated, although they are the most up-to-date figures in existence. The most recent comprehensive review of rateable values was cancelled by the government in 1979.

The abolition of Schedule A is only one of the tax benefits accruing to owner-occupiers. In addition, those taxpayers buying their homes on a mortgage are entitled to offset the mortgage interest charges against their tax liability and, as we have just noted, this concession 'costs' the Exchequer over £1·4 billion. While the maximum mortgage allowable is limited to £25,000, taxpayers are allowed to offset the interest charges against their marginal rate of tax. So again the mortgage relief for a taxpayer on the top rate of income tax is twice that accruing to the standard-rate taxpayer.

The third tax benefit for owner-occupiers is the exemption of the capital gains from taxation when the owner-occupier sells his main residence. The latest government White Paper on public expenditure puts the tax loss (or gain to individual taxpayers) at £2000 million.[9]

(iii) Insurance benefits

The granting of tax relief on life assurance results in another major erosion of the tax base. The cost of granting tax relief on life assurance premiums in 1979/80 is £430 million. Life assurance was devised in Britain over two centuries ago to help combat two very common predicaments from which many working-class families suffered – poverty through bereavement and poverty in old age. The basic idea was to create a fund from which a contributor could be paid an agreed annual income or a lump sum payment. Modern life assurance policies are not just concerned with death benefits or pension provisions. The industry has spread into most areas where people have to save regularly to buy a home, educate children or more generally to accumulate resources.

Tax relief on life assurance has been a long-established practice. Until fairly recently policy holders were entitled to tax relief on premiums paid under qualifying policies to the extent that the total of such premiums did not exceed one-sixth of their total income after charges, but before personal reliefs. The rate of relief was set at approximately half the standard rate of income tax. The policy holder paid the full amount of the premium to the insurance company and each individual taxpayer had to claim the relief direct from the Inland Revenue. The cost in Revenue staff-time in operating the scheme was put between 1000 and 1500 staff.

In his April 1976 Budget the then Chancellor, Denis Healey, announced changes in the administration of tax relief on life insurance premiums. In order to simplify administration, with a consequential saving of staff time, it was decided to introduce a system of relief by deduction. This scheme, which is now in operation, allows policy holders to deduct a set amount from each payment of an eligible premium, and in return the Life Offices receive corresponding direct payments from the Revenue to re imburse them for the reduction in their premium receipts. The entitlement to relief of up to one-sixth of total income has been retained but a new limit of £1500 per annum is allowed if this is greater. Relief is currently granted at half the standard rate, i.e. policy holders deduct 15 per cent from their total premiums.

The system of allowing deductions by taxpayers from their premiums has a small, important side-effect. In a moment we shall see how this tax benefit – like all others – most favours those on high incomes. But it also has an advantage for those at the other end of the income scale, and particularly those who don't pay tax. In this respect, life-insurance tax relief is unique. Under the system of deductions non-taxpayers also benefit as they are now entitled to deduct the relief. As with all other insurance holders, low-income non-taxpaying individuals are allowed an equal deduction of 15 per cent of the annual premium. The insurance company is then compensated by the government at the end of the year.

(iv) Tax-free social security benefits

The tax base is further eroded by exempting large numbers of social security benefits from tax. In the present circumstances of a very low tax threshold it makes sense to exempt some of these benefits from tax, but in a reformed tax system all income should be taxed so long as those with incomes at or below the poverty line are exempt from paying. At the moment, not all social security benefits are received tax free. Nine major benefits, including retirement pension, allowances to widows and mobility allowance, are liable to tax. In addition, the Thatcher government plans to tax almost all social security benefits as soon as the machinery is available to do so. In the meantime, it has introduced 'abating' rules so that the value of untaxed benefits have been reduced by five percentage points since November 1980. The government has yet to decide whether a further abatement will take place in the up-rating of benefits in November 1981. The benefits, now cut by five percentage points, include many of the main ones such as unemployment and sickness benefit, invalidity and injury benefit.

The reason for this abatement is primarily to save money from the social security budget thus helping to finance the tax cuts given to high income groups in the 1979 and 1980 Budgets. Had the abatement of 5 per cent been a genuine first move to taxing benefits (although this would still have been unjust, as in many cases those suffering cuts in benefit would not be paying tax), the government would have been able to guarantee to restore the abatements when they commence the normal taxing of benefits in 1982. The only guarantee given so far is that should funds be available the cuts made to invalidity benefit will be restored.

Who gets the tax benefits?

Something in excess of £20 billions – or about the same as is spent on the traditional welfare state – is awarded in tax benefits, and it is crucially important to observe who are the main beneficiaries of this second welfare state. As we shall see in a moment, the British data are far from complete. Fuller data are obtainable in other countries, and there is now a fairly extensive analysis undertaken in Canada of what they call 'the hidden welfare system'. Yet even here, only a minority of the tax benefits has been individually costed. The seventeen most important tax benefits cost in the region of $6·4 billion, and the forty other tax benefits add a further several billion dollars to the total. However, the seventeen alone:

> tell us a great deal about the hidden welfare system. To put this $6·4 billion figure into perspective, it was equal to well over one fifth of the entire Federal budget in 1974. It was four-and-a-half times the cost of the Olympic Games and nineteen times the total cost of the support/supplementation programmes (i.e. social security for the poor). It was enough money to have provided every family in Canada with an extra $1000 a month for food and clothing.[10]

Canada's National Council of Welfare provides a distributional analysis of who gains what from this second welfare state in that country. In the first place, the tax benefits are analysed according to income groups. On this the National Council of Welfare reports:

It would be difficult to imagine any direct and visible government expenditure programme that gave $244 to those with incomes of less than $5000 but $2427 – ten times as much – to those with incomes of $25,000 to $50,000 and $3990 to those who make over $50,000 a year. No government would dare propose such a programme. And yet the hidden welfare system does just that, and there is hardly a protest to be heard.

The report adds: 'The reason the hidden welfare system can get away with it is precisely because it is hidden. The low income taxpayer saving $200 cheers his saving – and remains oblivious to the $2000 saving granted to persons with five times his income.'[11]

The report also looks at the gain of the tax benefits according to the percentage of taxpayers in different income groups; this information is presented in Table 10. From this we can see that the top 11 per cent of taxpayers gained 33 per cent of the tax benefits whereas the bottom 70 per cent of taxpayers gained only 40 per cent.

Table 10   *Income taxpayers and gains from tax benefits (Canada)*

Income group	Percentage of all tax filers	Percentage of total benefits from the 17 tax subsidies
Under $5000	38·4	12·5
$5000–10,000	31·5	27·9
$10,000–15,000	18.7	26·5
$15,000–20,000	6·8	14·3
Over $20,000	4·6	18·8
	100·0	100·0

Source: The Hidden Welfare System, National Council of Welfare, Canada, 1976.

Unfortunately, we do not have such comprehensive information on the gains of the tax benefit welfare state in this country. Nevertheless, as a first move we can look at the value of the personal allowances to different income levels. This is given in Table 11, which shows how the value of the allowance is twice that for the higher-income groups on marginal tax rates of 60 per cent compared with those whose income is taxed at the standard rate. Likewise, the tax advantage is that much greater for households with two earners, particularly if one compares the value of the allowance of a family with one earner on the standard rate (who will quite likely have young children), and a two-wage household paying at the top rate of income tax – personal tax benefits valued at £642.24 and £2112.24 respectively.

The Royal Commission looked at the value of deductions for mortgage and other allowable interest payments according to income groups. This analysis included the value of retirement annuity premiums – which are examined in the following chapter. In 1975 the value of the deductions for allowable interest charges came to £648 for the top 1 per cent of taxpayers, £274 for the top 10 per cent of income taxpayers and a mere £12 for the bottom 10 per cent. In one important respect, of course, these figures underestimate the gains of the total tax benefit welfare state to high income earners. Those on higher incomes are more likely to buy their homes out of capital, or to inherit them, than to buy them on an ordinary mortgage from the building society. Nevertheless, the top 1 per cent still benefits at a ratio of 54 times more than the bottom 10 per cent.

The distributional effect of the tax allowance welfare state is again illustrated in the Royal Commission's updated analysis on mortgage interest relief. Table 12 gives the amount of revenue lost in mortgage interest relief for the financial year 1979/80, and these data are classified according to the income range of the recipient. That the tax benefit welfare state overwhelmingly benefits the rich can be seen from the second column. Those earning less than

Table II *Value of personal allowances to income taxpayers at each of the marginal rates of tax, 1980/1*

Tax unit	Marginal rate						
	30 per cent £	40 per cent £	45 per cent £	50 per cent £	55 per cent £	60 per cent £
Single person	412·36	550·16	618·80	687·44	756·08	825·24
Married person	642·24	858·00	965·12	1072·24	1179·88	1287·00
Two-wage earners	1054·60	1408·16	1583·92	1759·68	1937·96	2112·24

Source: reworked Inland Revenue data.

£3000 a year gained, on average, mortgage relief at £100 a year. Those at the other end of the income scale, earning in excess of £10,000 a year, gained an average tax benefit of £480. But these figures underestimate the gains to the rich. The number of taxpayers earning over £10,000 a year stood at 8·4 per cent, and yet 19 per cent of them were claiming mortgage interest relief compared to a little over 1 per cent of income taxpayers earning less than £2000 a year. And while those earning in excess of £10,000 a year made up less than 9 per cent of all taxpayers, they gained 34 per cent of all the mortgage interest tax benefit paid out during 1979/80.

Table 12 *Distributional impact of mortgage interest relief, 1979/80*

	Mortgage interest relief 1979/80[a]			
Total income range £	Average relief per mortgagor £	Numbers claiming relief (000s)[b]	Total relief £m	Total number of taxpayers per income range (000s)[b]
Under 1000	—	—	—	—
1000 – 2000	100	20	2	1600
2000 – 3000	100	140	14	2900
3000 – 5000	180	880	158	6500
5000 – 10,000	230	3340	768	8600
Over 10,000	480	1050	504	1800

[a] Relates to all mortgages.
[b] Counting married couples as one.

Sources: Inland Revenue; *Hansard,* 18 March 1980, c.149.

Tax relief on life assurance policies similarly benefits those on high incomes. Income taxpayers on over £10,000 a year in 1978/9 amounted to less than 4 per cent of all taxpayers, and yet they claimed 23 per cent of all tax relief given for life assurance policies. At the other end of the income scale, those earning under £3000 a year made up 30 per cent of taxpayers but gained only 7 per cent of tax relief given for life assurance policies.

The effect of reducing the average rate of tax for tax-payers benefiting most from the tax benefit welfare state can be seen if we include in our analysis not only mortgage tax relief but also superannuation payments and average life assurance (these latter two tax benefits are examined in more detail in Chapters 8 and 9). In order to appreciate the full effect of the tax changes brought about by the Thatcher government it is important to look at tax rates for 1978/9 and 1979/80. In public debate a taxpayer's marginal tax rate is used to illustrate the supposed crippling effect on initiative and the Draconian extent of redistribution of income from higher income earners. But the combination of the personal tax benefits together with the three probably most important other tax benefits – mortgage tax relief, superannuation and life assurance – have a dramatic effect on the average rate of tax paid by different taxpayers. In the last year of Labour government a single person on average earnings paid a marginal tax rate of 33 per cent and an average rate of around 13 per cent. Taxpayers paying a 65-per-cent marginal tax rate saw their rate of tax halved to an average of 32·5 per cent once the tax benefits had been taken into account.

The tax changes brought about in the first Budget of the Thatcher government made a dramatic change not only to the marginal but also the average rate of tax particularly for higher income groups. For the worker on average earnings, his marginal rate was reduced by 3 percentage points to 30 and his average rate was similarly reduced by 3 percentage points to 10·2 per cent. But the single person on £20,000 a year who previously paid a marginal rate of 65 per cent saw this reduce to 45 per cent and his average tax rate of 32·5 per cent cut to 25·7 per cent. Those paying the top rate of tax in the last year of the Labour government paid a marginal rate of 83 per cent and, if a single person claiming the range of tax allowances detailed above, an average rate of 49 per cent. One year later the same person on £35,000 a year paid a marginal rate of 60 per cent and an average rate of 36·7 per cent.

Conclusion

In this chapter we have been concerned with the second of five welfare states – the tax benefit welfare state. It differs in two fundamental respects from the traditional welfare state. In the first place, while it channels welfare to large sections of the population, those at the top end of the income scale are the biggest beneficiaries. The main effect, therefore, of the tax benefit welfare state is to widen rather than to diminish inequalities. Second, unlike the traditional welfare state whose growth is contained by the government's attempts to control public expenditure, the tax benefit system remains unaffected by any restrictions whatsoever and each of the tax concessions is a blank cheque signed by the Chancellor. The effect of the tax allowance welfare state is not only to reduce marginal tax rates but average ones as well, and particularly for those at the top end of the income scale. While this chapter has been concerned with those tax benefits which accrue directly to taxpayers as individuals, the following three chapters will examine the extent to which the tax system supports the three other welfare states.

8. The Company Welfare State

Living standards are not only determined by the size of one's wage or salary cheque together with entitlements to welfare and tax benefits. They are also affected by those benefits which derive from unearned incomes and company welfare. In this chapter we shall look at the range and growth in welfare provided by both private and state-owned companies, and we examine first the extent of company pension, sick pay and insurance provisions which exist in addition to state benefits. The second part of the chapter goes on to look at those benefits such as company cars, loans, shares and houses which a growing number of companies provide for their higher paid employees. We shall also be examining the two-fold distributional impact of company welfare in the way it helps to spread the tax load of high income earners over what can sometimes be decades, while appreciably increasing the difference in living standards between high and low income earners.

Extent of company welfare

One of the best sources of information on the extent of company welfare is the Royal Commission on the Distribution of Income and Wealth, which made a distinction between two kinds of company welfare provisions. The first they called 'welfare' benefits and under this heading the Commission put free or subsidized meals, sports facilities and goods at discount prices, rent-free housing and other benefits in kind. The second form of welfare they described as 'other' benefits and here they included a company car in cases where its use is not directly related to the job, free or cheap loans, bonuses and profit sharing. The Royal Commission went on to observe that benefits in the first group are generally available to all employees in a firm, and while their existence was often a result of historical accident, their recent growth was the result of negotiations between employers and the unions. On the other hand, the 'other' benefits are provided 'to attract and retain staff, and have expanded considerably over the years of incomes policy to combat the narrowing of the margin of executive rewards caused by the tax structure and pay restraint.'[1]

This justification for these additional 'perks' is not, however, borne out by the facts. As we have seen in Chapters 1, 6 and 7, neither the macro data on the distribution of income, nor the analysis of the changing burden of taxation, suggest a significant narrowing of the gap between the bottom and top wage and salary earners during recent years. However, under the cover of supposed narrowing of differentials between managerial workers and the rest, the company welfare state has expanded considerably in the past few years and most particularly for those on high earnings.

In 1974 a British Institute of Management (BIM) survey of 455 companies found that 72 per cent provided company welfare benefits in order 'to attract and retain employees', 59 per cent saw company welfare as a means of providing 'conditions of employment which compare well with other companies'; and 39 per cent saw company welfare as 'a way to motivate employees'. The survey also interviewed 183 managers who described such benefits as 'an expression of the company's concern for the welfare of employees', a 'necessary means of competing with other companies in the labour market', as well as being 'a means of recognizing the employees' security and status within the company'.[2]

Ironically, however, the tax advantages that welfare benefits bring to the company are countered to some extent by the difficulties they cause. Thus, evidence to the Royal Commission suggests that, with the exception of company cars and medical insurance, other benefits are 'forced upon [firms] by the demands made by existing or potential employees, and by their obvious advantages under present tax legislation in terms of reducing labour costs'. Thus, one firm of consultants submitting a survey of twenty companies as evidence to the Royal Commission listed the main advantage of fringe benefits as a means of reducing employees' tax liabilities, but reported the companies disliking them as being difficult to administer, having limited incentive value and causing some friction among those employees who were not recipients of the full range of company welfare.[3] But, whether companies like or dislike the growth of company welfare, growth there has been over the past decade – particularly in relation to pension, sick-pay schemes and housing provisions.

(i) Pensions

The provision of company pensions advanced rapidly in the years up to 1967. In 1936, 2·6 million workers were members of company pension schemes. This total jumped to 6·2 million by 1953, rising to 8 million three years later. By 1963 the total had topped 11·1 million and the numbers of workers in company pension schemes reached an all-time peak of 12·2 million in 1967. This total fell to 11·1 million in 1971, rising to 11·5 million in 1975. Overwhelmingly, membership of company pension schemes has been among male workers and this is the first of a number of distinguishing characteristics. They accounted for 2·1 million of the 2·6 members in 1936 and even by 1975, 8·7 million of the 11·5 million workers covered by company pension arrangements were male employees.

A second major difference in coverage is between manual

and non-manual workers. Although there are more manual than non-manual workers, only 4·7 million out of a total of 11·1 million workers covered in 1971 were manual workers. This total was improved somewhat by 1975 with an extra three-quarters of a million manual workers in the public sector offsetting a decline of a quarter of a million manual workers in the private sector.

A third major difference is between workers in the public and private sector. Pension coverage, overall, is much higher in the public sector. In 1975 it stood at 74 per cent – compared with 38 per cent in the private sector; 84 per cent of men in the public sector (compared with 52 per cent in the private sector) were covered by occupational pension schemes. Significantly, however, women workers fare even better in the public sector, where 59 per cent (compared with only 17 per cent in the private sector) are covered by occupational pension schemes.

Despite recent increases, almost $7\frac{1}{2}$ million workers were outside company pension schemes in 1975. Overwhelmingly, these workers were concentrated in the private sector – a total of 5,560,000.[4] Moreover, while workers are covered by company pension arrangements, a vast majority of pensions in payment are for small amounts. The latest figures show that 1,280,000 of the 2,950,000 pensions in payment were for £5 a week or less, while 63 per cent of all pensions were £10 a week or less.[5] In stark contrast are the pensions paid to top salary earners, where salaries are inflated during the last years of service in order to increase significantly the living standards of recipients during retirement. As the Royal Commission commented:

Occupational schemes are important in the context of higher incomes from employment, particularly for employees approaching the end of their careers, since a major reason for seeking and granting salary increases for those bearing the highest rate of tax is that they lead to improved superannuation provisions which carry associated tax advantages.[6]

The tax advantages work in the following ways. Pension schemes defer income, which would currently be subject to high marginal rates of taxation, to a future date when the recipient will most probably be on a lower level of income and therefore paying lower marginal rates of taxation. Moreover, so long as the scheme is approved by the Inland Revenue, both the employers' and employees' contributions are excluded from income before tax is levied, i.e., it reduces their tax liability. In addition, the increasing value from the pension fund's investments are exempt from tax, and tax is only charged once the pensions are drawn. The recipient's tax load is further reduced by the payment of lump sums. The Royal Commission gave examples of high income earners during the period when the highest marginal rate of tax on earned incomes stood at 83 per cent. These arrangements legitimately allowed the incidence of tax on the combined value of the occupational pension and the lump-sum payment to reduce a marginal rate from 83 per cent to 62 per cent. Those on marginal rates of 75 per cent when in work were able to postpone part of their consumption by way of pension contributions and pay tax at a 56-per-cent marginal rate on their retirement income.[7]

A further inequality in pensions arises from the formula by which pensions are calculated. We have already noted that one of the justifications for excessive wage increases for higher income earners approaching retirement is to boost the recipient's pension. While 90 per cent of non-manual members of private sector schemes had their pensions based on final salaries, the proportion among manual members so treated was only about two-thirds. 'Consequently over one million of the one and a quarter million members who could only expect a pension based on some other figure – either a fixed amount or a fraction of average salary throughout service in most cases – were manual workers.'[8]

Of course it is true that for many manual workers, income tails off as retirement approaches. Some pension schemes therefore allow employees in both the public and private sectors to have their pensions based on the best three years or even a single best year in a period of up to the thirteen years prior to their retirement. But even here inflation eats away at any advantage which might have been gained by lower paid workers. Peak earnings during the decade or so prior to retirement will have been greatly devalued by the inflation over the past few years, let alone the last decade. Hence the advantage to high salary earners whose income rises to a peak as they retire and who can draw their pensions based on their salary immediately prior to retirement.

(ii) Sick pay

Similar discrepancies between manual and non-manual workers, and between male and female workers, are also evident in the protection offered by sick-pay schemes, and this pattern is further complicated by industrial and regional variations. In 1974 the DHSS carried out a major survey of company sick-pay schemes which revealed that there had been a significant increase in the proportion both of men and of women employees covered by company sick-pay arrangements. In 1961, 57 per cent of employees were covered by company schemes and this proportion had risen to 73 per cent in 1970. The 1974 survey showed an 80-per-cent coverage, but with major industrial variations. For example, whereas coverage for male workers in coal and petroleum industries was at 96·7 per cent, and 95·1 per cent in mining and quarrying, coverage fell to 50 per cent for male workers in leather, leather goods and fur industries. A similar pattern is discernible for women workers. In coal and petroleum products, where there are few women workers, coverage was 100 per cent, but it was only 40 per cent in leather, leather goods and fur manufacture, where women are much more numerous.[9]

Differences in coverage were also found between manual and non-manual workers. While over 90 per cent of both men and women non-manual workers were covered by company sick-pay provisions in 1974, only three-quarters of manual male workers and less than 60 per cent of all women manual workers were covered. Sick-pay cover also varied in different parts of the country. For men workers the highest proportion covered (88·7 per cent) was in the South East and the lowest proportion (66·6 per cent) was in the West Midlands. For married women, 89·1 per cent were covered by company sick-pay provisions in the South East but only 64 per cent in Yorkshire and Humberside. Once again, the highest coverage of company sick-pay arrangements for single women was in the South East (92·5 per cent), the lowest in Wales (57·5 per cent).[10]

The report also noted three major differences in the treatment of lower paid employees in the rules operating company sick-pay benefits. At the present time national insurance sick pay is not paid for the first three days of illness. The DHSS survey showed that while benefit was paid at the onset of sickness for almost 93 per cent of non-manual men and 94 per cent of non-manual women, just under 57 per cent of manual men and a little over 67 per cent of manual women workers were paid company sick-pay benefit from the first day off work.

There was also a significant difference in the length of time company sick-pay benefit was paid for manual and non-manual workers. The report showed that, on the whole, manual workers were limited to a shorter period of entitlement than were non-manual men. More non-manual than manual male workers, for example, were entitled to sick pay for 52 weeks and over (26·7 per cent compared to 15 per cent) and similar differences were to be found for women workers. Differences were also to be found in the size of payments. More than twice the percentage of non-manual men, compared to manual male workers, gained their full pay without any deductions of the state benefit. The report showed that there were similar differences between manual and non-manual women workers.[11]

A further inequality in the provision of company sick-pay benefits was highlighted in one of the later Royal Commission reports: 72 per cent of full-time manual men, compared with only 33 per cent of full-time non-manual men, had to serve a qualifying period before gaining eligibility for benefit. As the Royal Commission went on to observe, 'The qualifying period is one factor reducing the likelihood of coverage for manual workers, as it is in the case of occupational pension schemes.'[12]

These findings are immensely important when we come on to consider the proposals the government has now made for reforming the national insurance sick-pay scheme whereby employers will be responsible for paying sickness benefit for the first weeks of illness. Indeed, it is ironic that this development of the company welfare state is being used as the reason for dismantling part of the traditional welfare state. In support of its proposals the government have pointed out that 10 million claims for state sickness benefit are made each year but that only a very small proportion of people who qualify for benefit draw it for any length of time. While no payment is made for the first three days of incapacity, 60 per cent of those who qualify for sickness benefit are back at work at the end of a fortnight, 80 per cent within a month and 90 per cent within six weeks.[13]

On the basis of this kind of information the government is proposing the abolition of state sickness benefit for up to eight weeks in a tax year. In order to 'simplify' the scheme and thereby make the system easily administerable for employers (as well as to make a £⅓ billion saving in public expenditure), the government is in the process of abolishing the earnings-related supplement to sickness benefit (plus the supplement to other national insurance benefits as well).

The danger for lower paid workers in these proposals is obvious. Large numbers of them are not actually covered by company welfare provisions when sick. While the government asserts that 'there are relatively few employees who have to serve waiting days' for sickness benefit,[14] those who are are heavily concentrated among the ranks of manual workers.

These proposals are still under consideration. In the meantime, it is important to record that from all available evidence, the company welfare state widens inequalities rather than reduces them, and the partial dismantling of the state's sickness benefit scheme will widen these differences still further. This unequal treatment is reinforced by the range of company welfare which is provided almost exclusively for those on high incomes.

Top people's welfare

(i) Cars

For many, the company car represents the most conspicuous example of top people's benefits. But it is only one of a number of benefits ranging from direct financial help to housing and health insurance.

In 1974 a BIM survey asked companies their reasons for providing cars. The results showed that 'the essential need for business travel' and 'the fringe benefit requirements of employees' were major factors and that 'overall, companies rate the fringe benefit aspect as more important'.[15]

The survey carried out by Inbucon in 1978 shows a rise in the number of higher paid employees with the full use of a company car; from 55·2 per cent in 1973 to 67·4 per cent in 1978. This disguises a marked difference in access to a company car even among those who are in the higher income brackets. An earlier AIC/Inbucon survey found that 97 per cent of managing directors had sole use of a company car, and this figure declined steadily with status to 20·5 per cent of middle management (who were the

Table 13 *Top people's company welfare*

Fringe benefits other than retirement pensions, 1973/8						
Benefit	Proportion of the sample receiving benefit in:					
	1973 %	1974 %	1975 %	1976 %	1977 %	1978 %
Top hat pension	23·6	19·3	20·3	19·4	15·2	15·6
Full use of company car	55·2	62·0	60·6	62·3	63·8	67·4
Allowance for regular use of own car	14·5	12·3	12·8	10·7	8·6	8·3
Subsidized lunches	65·0	64·2	63·6	67·3	65·9	68·6
Subsidized housing	1·4	0·9	1·1	1·0	0·7	1·0
Assistance with house purchase	6·3	4·7	6·4	5·9	7·4	8·0
Life assurance						
up to and incl 3 × salary	—	53·1	57·9	58·8	61·6	62·4
exceeding 3 × salary	—	22·2	25·5	27·5	23·9	26·7
Free medical insurance	26·4	30·1	37·9	37·3	38·8	44·1
Share option scheme	2·5	4·2	4·3	5·3	3·7	6·0
Share purchase scheme	5·1	4·3	3·5	4·1	3·3	3·4
Low interest loans	—	—	—	7·2	9·7	9·6
Bonus	30·2	32·6	31·1	33·9	33·3	37·1

Source: Survey of executive salaries and fringe benefits, Inbucon, 1978; reproduced from Royal Commission, Report No. 8, Table 9.9.

lowest rank covered in the survey). The likelihood of having a car provided also increased with salary – from 79 per cent for those on salaries in 1975 of between £5000 and £9999 to over 92 per cent for those on salaries in excess of £10,000.

The trend towards providing company cars continues. As far back as 1974 a GLC survey revealed that more than one-third of a million cars circulating daily in London were to some degree subsidized by companies[16] and if the recent Incomes Data Services (IDS) report on fringe benefits is reflective of more general trends, this total is much higher today. IDS's survey shows that the provision of company cars reflects the company's pay hierarchy. Companies made provision for two groups of workers; those who needed a car for their job and those whose status in the company required a car. IDS report, for example, that the Automobile Association's rules are for a director to be allowed a Rover, regional personnel officers a Cortina 1600, while the sales force gain Escort 1300s. Staff earning less than £7500 per annum pay £10 a month for the use of the car, but have their petrol and oil expenses reimbursed. Management on higher salary levels receive a 'perk' car and pay no expenses.[17]

The value of having a company car depends crucially on a whole series of assumptions. For executives on a salary of £15,853 per annum in 1975, using the company car for private motoring for a third of a total mileage of 10,000 miles, the value of this fringe benefit in terms of an increase of pre-tax salary was £641 before interest charges on the loan of buying the car, and £1101 once interest charges were included. However, if the company car was used exclusively for 10,000 miles of private motoring then the value of the benefit rose substantially, up to £2039 before interest charges or £3699 once interest charges were included.[18]

Updating these figures for the same salary in 1980/1 following the 1980 Budget changes shows that it would require a gross increase of salary of £2492 in order to finance the value of this fringe benefit out of taxable income. If all the 10,000 miles of the car are undertaken for private motoring then the value rises to £4901 and the increase in gross salary which would be required to pay for a car out of taxable income stands at £6698.

The value of a company car is subjected to tax in only a notional sense. It would be difficult for the Inland Revenue to undertake complicated calculations to ascertain the value to each individual taxpayer. The Revenue therefore lays down a scale of imputed values. This varies with the cost of the car and the car's horsepower. In the example cited above, the car's cost was put at £14,129 and the calculation applied to a car over four years old. For new cars costing over £12,000, an imputed value of £880 is given in the current year (1980/1) and this will rise to £1050 in 1981/2. For cars over four years old the imputed value is reduced by a third. While this scale rate is well below the actual value, it is this sum which is added to total income and then charged at the marginal rate. For a car, therefore, where business use is 'not insubstantial', in the current year with an imputed value of £880, it would cost the tax-payer paying at a marginal rate of 45 per cent £396 per year (or with a car over four years old, £263). The scale rate is at present reduced by one-half if the car is used for 25,000 miles a year or more on business. Moreover, from 1981/2 the qualifying mileage will be reduced to 18,000. Other changes will be made for cars which are used for 'insubstantial' business use.

(ii) *Life assurance and health insurance*

Table 13 also shows an increase in provision of life assurance for top salary earners: 53·1 per cent of executives were covered in 1974, and this total had risen to 62·4 per cent in 1978. As the Royal Commission noted, assurance appears as a fringe benefit in two forms. The life assurance is usually an integral part of superannuation arrangements, and private medical insurance is also made through BUPA and similar schemes. The advantage of paying this premium through the company is the size of discounts it gains for placing block orders. Free medical insurance for top salary earners has risen at a faster rate than has life assurance. The Inbucon 1978 survey shows a growth from 26·4 per cent of top paid employees covered in 1973, rising to 44·1 per cent in 1978. Again, both life assurance and medical insurance widen inequalities rather than narrow them.

The latest information shows an extension of employees covered by health insurance schemes. Figures for 1978 released by the three leading provincial associations – British United Provident Association (BUPA), Private Patients Plan and Western Provident Association – which between them account for 98 per cent of all medical insurance, show a membership rise in 1978 of 11 per cent. Interpreting these figures, the *Financial Times* correspondent, Eric Short, observed that there are now nearly 650,000 subscribers in group health schemes where the employer pays most or all of the contribution. Since under many schemes benefit also covers members of the employee's household, about 2 million people will have health insurance under company schemes.[19] Practically all the firms reported in the IDS study giving coverage to senior staff with private health insurance admit their families to the scheme as well. For example, Abbott Laboratories Limited reported that senior staff have free membership of BUPA for themselves and their spouses. Other staff may join BUPA at the discount rate.[20]

(iii) Housing

The history of company welfare provision to help employees purchase their own homes shows a chequered growth. The Inbucon survey listed 6·3 per cent of top employees in 1973 gaining this welfare benefit, falling the following year, but rising to 8 per cent by 1978. A later survey listed 19 per cent of companies surveyed as providing housing loans for their employees. In 1974 BIM's survey gave more details, showing that 39 per cent of companies questioned provided bridging loans for their employees, while 70 per cent provided guarantees to building societies. Bridging at the present time, provided at a nil rate of interest, results in the following benefits to employees. On an average-priced house (£23,500 in April 1980) a bridging loan for one month amounts to a welfare benefit valued at £300. If the loan lasts for a year the benefit's value rises to £3500. These benefits are free of tax.

(iv) Loans

Low interest loans are one of the more recently established company welfare benefits. The Inbucon surveys show that the number of higher paid employees receiving such a benefit rose from 7·2 per cent in 1976 to 9·7 per cent a year later, falling fractionally in the following year. The Top Salaries Review Body in its sixth report gave details of the number of board members and senior executives receiving low-interest loans. The percentage of board members in September 1973 was 7·8 per cent and senior executives 11·6 per cent, while the average size loan for the first category was £28,096 and £9233 for the latter group. The average interest payment for board members stood at 1·4 per cent and senior executives 1·3. (At this time bank rates stood at 11·25 per cent.) The Royal Commission reworked these data to look at the average saving of interest on such loans. They found that in 1973 the average loan to board members saved the recipient £1436 in interest, whereas the senior executive's loan saved interest payments each year of £1327.

Some companies offer loans to employees for a whole range of needs, and some provide personal loans in cases of financial crises. IDS reports, for example, the Automobile Association allowing loans in such circumstances up to a limit of £200. Grindlays Bank allows staff to borrow up to 15 per cent of their salaries at 5-per cent interest, but these loans must be repaid over a maximum of three years. Other forms of financial help are given to employees to help to pay for education fees. Fisons Limited allow employees with twelve months' or more service to receive a discretionary *ex-gratia* grant towards the grant of higher education for their children.[21] Top employees of other companies are offered help in meeting the costs of the school fees for their children.

Apart from the significant savings on interest charges, loans from an employer to an employee will often be for a greater amount than the individual employee could raise in the private market. The company benefit is therefore twofold: loans are gained at a considerably reduced rate of interest and the employee's access to capital funds is significantly increased. The Royal Commission notes that while access can clearly be of great value to the recipient, 'there is no practical way in which it can be quantified, either for loans or for other access benefits.' The Royal Commission adds that such loans were more common in the finance sector of industry and that they 'are common at all levels in that sector, and not confined to higher income earners'.[22] One example of the range of company welfare in the finance sector is given in the Select Committee on Nationalized Industries' examination of the Bank of England. The Committee reported that company welfare benefits offered to employees include home loans at 2 or $2\frac{1}{2}$ per cent, twenty-year loans at 3 per cent to pay for private education, interest-free loans for season tickets, personal loans at 3 per cent and a non-contributory pension scheme.[23]

(v) Shares

Because of tax changes, the popularity of share purchase schemes has declined for, as the Royal Commission records: 'Fringe benefits involving company shares are very varied, and have changed considerably over time in response to changes in tax legislation.'[24] While there are two types of scheme, the share option scheme and the share acquisition scheme, each form of company share-issuing covers a wide variety of practices. The share option scheme is one characterized by the employee having the option of purchasing up to a certain number of company shares in the future at a price fixed when the option is being granted. The popularity of this form of share scheme declined after the 1966 Budget when share option gains were generally taxed as income at the time the option had been given to the employee. Relaxations on this ruling in the 1972 and 1973 Budgets were again reversed in the 1974 Finance Act. On the other hand, share acquisition schemes enable an employee to acquire company shares, and any difference between the value of the shares on acquisition and the price paid for them counts as income.

While there is no comprehensive information which would allow estimates of the value of either scheme to employee participants, the AIC/Inbucon 1975 survey did provide data on the level of participation in the schemes at different levels within the company hierarchy. It reported that 11·5 per cent of managing directors had benefited from the share option scheme, together with 6·9 per cent of the share purchase scheme. The average for all companies was 4·3 per cent in the option share scheme and 3·5 per cent in the share purchase scheme. Like managing directors, secretaries of public companies had a higher participation rate of 8·5 per cent for both schemes.

(vi) Food

Although the benefits of free or subsidized foods are more widely spread than most other company benefits, the inequality in reward is still very much in evidence. Meals in employers' canteens are free of tax and this tax exemption applies whether the meals are provided for manual workers or directors. The 1968 *DE Labour Costs Survey* found that while only 8·7 per cent of employers provided luncheon vouchers, 59·2 per cent provided 'canteens, restaurants and other food services'. The 1973 BIM survey reported that 37 per cent of companies in their sample provided free luncheon vouchers and three-quarters of companies provided a canteen or restaurant. The same survey showed that only 8 per cent of companies provided meals at cost, while the vast majority served subsidized meals to their employees.

Ironically, the chance of gaining a free meal increases with status: 5 per cent of manual workers gain free meals compared with 20 per cent for top managers and, of course, tax-free benefits also are more valuable to higher than lower income earners. The IDS study shows subsidized meals as being one of the most common forms of company welfare, and that the higher the person is in the company's hierarchy the greater the size of the subsidy. The Thomas Cook Group, for example, have subsidized canteens in Peterborough and London where the average meal of three courses costs around 75p. Staff pay only for the cost of the food, but those staff at the top of the hierarchy have free meals in the management dining-room.[25]

The Royal Commission tried to estimate the *total* value of company welfare for five employees positioned at different points in the company hierarchy in July 1975. They took salaries ranging from almost £5500 to over £24,000. The cost to an employer of superannuation and fringe benefits for these employees ranged from £988 a year up to £6909 for the highest paid. The percentage added to salary costs for providing company welfare amounted to 18 per cent for the employee on £5500 to 29 per cent for the highest paid employee in the example.[26]

Conclusion

Company welfare benefits have grown considerably in range over the past few years and we have seen that for some employees the company welfare state now extends not only to pension and insurance provision but also to cheap loans, assistance with house purchasing, free medical insurance, share purchase schemes and the provision of a company car. Not all these benefits are universally shared – not even among top people. Some, like cars, are strictly hierarchical, the larger cars going to top salary earners; others, like loans or shares, are taken up by top executives and are restricted according to the type of jobs; others, like meals, are technically available to the workforce as a whole, but even here, what is offered often reflects relative status within the organization. Even the most generous of company welfare benefits favours highly paid workers, discriminates against manual workers, and so increases class differences.

9. Inherited Power and Welfare

Information presented in the earlier part of the book on the distribution of income and wealth is once again relevant to the discussion in this and the following chapter. Chapter 1 was concerned with plotting the unequal distribution of wealth and showing how limited had been any redistribution to lower income groups. We are now concerned with looking at that aspect of wealth which gives rise to what is generally called unearned income, i.e. those assets which generate income, rent or dividend payments to the owner. We shall be particularly concerned with which groups are in receipt, and with the value of this unearned welfare.

At the turn of the century a group of churchmen produced a book which they called *Property: Its Duties and Rights*. In his chapter on the 'Evolution of Property', L. T. Hobhouse distinguished between the two functions of property which he listed as 'the control over things, which gives freedom and security, and the control over persons through things, which gives power to the owner.'[1]

The unequal distribution of property, which gives the owner 'control over persons' as well as unearned income, was noted by studies carried out in the 1950s including that conducted by H. F. Lydall and D. G. Tipping. Examining the composition of portfolios in 1954, they found that the wealthiest 1 per cent of the population owned 81 per cent of company stocks and shares; the top 5 per cent, 96 per cent of company stocks and shares; and this percentage rose to 98 per cent for the wealthiest 10 per cent of the community. A similar, though not so extreme concentration of holdings was found in land, building and trade assets. Here the top 1, 5 and 10 per cent owned 28 per cent, 58 per cent and 74 per cent respectively of these assets. The same groups owned 42 per cent, 71 per cent and 83 per cent respectively of government securities.[2]

The concentration of wealth in certain forms by the very rich was again highlighted in the findings of J. R. S. Revell's study on the wealth portfolios of men aged between fifty-five and sixty-four. Whereas men with assets of £3000 had 20 per cent of those assets in cash or bank deposits, those with assets of over £250,000 had only 8 per cent of their assets in this form of wealth. However, whereas the £3000 man had only 3 per cent of his portfolio in company securities, the man with assets of over £250,000 had 38 per cent of his portfolio in company shares. The wealth of those at the bottom end of the income scale was then, as now, much more likely to be in the form of cash, bank deposits, building society deposits and the part ownership of an owner-occupied house.[3]

Additional evidence on the spread of asset holdings between different groups was provided by a survey carried out in 1968 for the Association of Building Societies. This showed that whereas manual workers and pensioners made up almost 70 per cent of the population, they accounted for only 15 per cent of all shareholders. In addition, they held 64 per cent of all national savings bank accounts and a total of 74 per cent of Trustee Savings Bank accounts.[4]

The unequal distribution of property, which gives power over other people as well as an unearned income, still exists and can be seen from more recent data. Indeed, one way of distinguishing which assets are likely to be owned by the very wealthy is to consider which are likely to give power over third parties. While National Savings Certificates and Premium Bonds are no doubt of considerable importance to their owners, their ownership can hardly be considered as directly affecting the lives of other people. Likewise, while about a half of all wealth was represented by buildings in 1975, such wealth, while giving considerable power of choice to the owner, again does not directly affect the lives of other people – except for that small minority of residential property which is rented.

The same cannot be said for the ownership of shares and debentures in companies or the ownership of land. These are key assets in the exercise of power over other people (even if that power is operated through third parties) and the ownership of these assets is markedly concentrated in the hands of the very wealthy. For example, of all shares and debentures in companies, 41·1 per cent were owned by wealth holders in the £50,000 to £200,000 range in 1975, while those wealth holders with assets over £200,000 owned 30·6 per cent of shares and debentures. The ownership of land is similarly concentrated. Those owning wealth valued between £50,000–£200,000 and over £200,000 owned 43·2 and 27·4 per cent respectively of all land in 1975.

An equally important way of examining which wealth is owned by different groups of the population is to examine the composition of assets for different wealth holders. Such an analysis shows that for those listed with net wealth of £5000 but less than £10,000 in 1976, a fraction over half (50·2 per cent) of that wealth was to be found in dwellings and a further 20·4 per cent in life policies, and only 0·5 per cent in land, 0·9 per cent in listed ordinary shares (including unit trusts) and 0·2 per cent in company securities. In contrast, asset holders with wealth valued in excess of £200,000 had only 13·1 per cent of their wealth in dwellings and a mere 2·7 per cent in life policies, but had invested 20 per cent of their wealth in land, 14·3 per cent in company securities and 21·8 per cent in listed ordinary shares.[5]

Unearned income is heavily concentrated in few hands for the simple reason that it is linked with only certain forms of wealth holdings. Of course, the living standards of an owner-occupier are increased as a result of the imputed rent derived from the building which he occupies. Similarly, durable consumer capital goods also increase the living standards of those lucky enough to own them, just as the receipt of an occupational or state pension makes a major difference to the lifestyle of the pensioner. Income from these assets excluded from the traditional calculations on unearned income but, as Tony Atkinson notes, 'the figures also exclude an important element of income accruing to the top wealth holders – capital gains – and in quantitive terms these may be at least as significant.' In Table 14, on the percentage of investment income going to different income groups, we see that unearned income is heavily concentrated among those who are at the top end of the income scale. Even allowing for the way the

Table 14 *Distribution of earned and investment income, 1975/6*

Income group		(1) Earned income (£bn)	(2) (1) as percentage of total earned income	(3) Investment income (£m)	(4) (3) as percentage of total investment income
Top 1	per cent	3280	4·8	1080	27·6
2–5	per cent	7320	10·7	743	19·0
6–10	per cent	7050	10·3	328	8·4
Top 10	per cent	17,600	25·8	2150	55·0
11–20	per cent	11,600	17·0	383	9·8
21–30	per cent	9440	13·8	297	7·6
31–40	per cent	8070	11·8	250	6.4
41–50	per cent	6360	9·3	239	6·1
51–60	per cent	5060	7·4	203	5·2
61–70	per cent	3760	5·5	172	4·4
71–80	per cent	2800	4·1	109	2·8
81–90	per cent	2120	3·1	70·4	1·8
91–100	per cent	1500	2·2	35·2	0·9
		68,400	100·0	3910	100·0

Source: Royal Commission data, reworked.

table is computed, as Tony Atkinson suggested about an earlier series of data, 'the higher return earned by the wealthy would quite possibly turn out to be a genuine phenomenon.'[6]

The evidence in the table shows that the already unequal distribution of earned income is only one part of the inequality in the share of total income in the community. And while there has been a reduction in the inequalities in unearned income over the past few years, the reductions have been small and have hardly affected those at the bottom of the income distribution. Indeed, the latest available data show that the richest 1 per cent of income groups, while commanding 4·8 per cent of all earned income (£3280 m), secured 27·6 per cent of investment or unearned income (a further £1080 m). Similarly, the top 2 to 5 per cent in the income group, while gaining 10·7 per cent of earned income, were also allotted 19 per cent of investment income. As a group, the top 10 per cent of income earners gained 25·8 per cent of all earned income in 1975/6, together with a staggering 55 per cent of all investment or unearned income.

One possible justification for the maldistribution of unearned income is that people should be free to forego consumption at the present time (i.e., to save) so that they can use these savings as a form of income at a later date. If the present distribution of personal incomes were more even, this argument might hold some force. Moreover, even in an egalitarian society, one would expect older members of the community to have larger assets than younger members. But the present distribution of wealth in this country can hardly be explained in terms of personal savings.[7] On the basis of their calculations, the Royal Commission observed that one would expect the top 1 per cent to own something between 3 and 7 per cent of personal wealth instead of the 22·5 per cent given by the Inland Revenue for 1974, while the top 2 to 5 per cent of wealth owners could expect to possess between 11 and 17 per cent of wealth instead of the 21 per cent recorded by the Inland

Revenue. Similarly, the Royal Commission estimated that the poorest 80 per cent of the population could expect to own over 40 per cent of the wealth if the distribution of wealth was determined by savings, instead of the 23·7 per cent allotted to this group in the Inland Revenue figures.[8]

There are indeed other explanations for the accumulation of wealth, and particularly that wealth which gives rise to unearned income. One key factor is the role of inheritance. The Royal Commission showed that 75 per cent of the richest 1 per cent's wealth was accounted for by inheritance. Transmitted wealth accounted for 52 per cent of the wealth holdings of the richest 2 to 5 per cent of the population. Not surprisingly, given the distribution of wealth, the bottom 80 per cent inherited next to nothing.

The importance of inheritance in explaining the massively unequal distribution of wealth has been established by the work of Professor Harbury and David Hitchens. Harbury looked at the wealth of matched pairs of individuals from different generations of the same family, and commented:

> If there is one firm conclusion that seems to stand out ... it is that inheritance is the major determinant of wealth inequality. The proportions of top wealth leaders who are preceded by wealthy fathers since the mid-fifties was shown, on what might be regarded as conservative assumptions, to be in excess of 60 per cent. Nearly three-quarters of the rich men in the sample had fathers whose fortunes were ten or more times the minimum needed to qualify for inclusion in the top 10 per cent of the wealth distribution. In contrast, on the assumption of no association between the wealth of fathers and sons one would expect less than 1 per cent to have been born to rich fathers.[9]

Professor Harbury's research showed that the wealth of large numbers of those who had not inherited considerable assets from their fathers could be explained by the wealth their wives inherited from their fathers. And he concluded by observing, 'without question, the firmest conclusion to emerge from this study is that inheritance is the major determinant of wealth inequality.'[10]

Conclusion

This chapter has made a distinction between wealth which increases the status and dignity of the owner and that which gives power over other people. This second form of wealth is not only highly unequally distributed but results in an unearned income and so helps guarantee the owner a higher standard of living. In this sense, unearned income acts in the same way as do traditional welfare benefits, although their distribution is almost totally limited to the top echelons of society and the benefits are infinitely more generous At the same time, those who are on high earnings not only gain considerable tax and company welfare benefits but are able to buy themselves into the private market welfare state. We now turn to examine the two major private welfare states in a little more detail.

10. The Private Market Welfare State

The continued gross inequalities in earned income, supported, as we have just seen, by an even more unequal distribution of unearned income, ensures that top earners enjoy high living standards and the option of buying themselves into the private market welfare state. Two aspects of the private market are considered here. The first is the growth of private health care both within and outside the NHS. The forms by which public subsidies are given to this welfare state are examined, together with the way in which this welfare state locks into the company welfare state. The second private welfare state examined here is the private provision of education. The gains in life chances for the pupils, and the means by which public schools are funded from the taxpayer's purse, are considered in the second half of the chapter.

Private welfare state: health care

Two of the most important human commodities available are health care and education. Both contribute immeasurably to personal and family welfare and both can be bought at a price. The unequal distribution of earned and unearned income, reinforced by key tax concessions, allows some people the income with which to buy private health care. The Royal Commission on the National Health Service listed the five main forms in which this private market welfare state operates. Here we are concerned only with the two main areas, which cover the health care provided in private hospitals and nursing homes, together with its provision within the National Health Service.

(i) Care outside the NHS

Looking at the size of private health service expenditure, Michael Lee has shown that while the total budget on private care has increased by 7·9 per cent in constant prices in the years 1970 to 1976, there is a marked difference between the growth in expenditure in the NHS and the independent hospitals. Lee shows that over the same period of time expenditure on private care in NHS hospitals rose on average by 0·1 per cent while that in the private hospitals increased at a rate of 13·7 per cent.

Lee draws attention to the 'distinct shift' in expenditure from NHS private beds to independent hospitals since 1974, which 'can be simply attributed to the uncertainties arising then on private beds in NHS hospitals'.[1] One explanation is that industrial action affecting NHS hospitals and private beds clearly affected trends from 1974 and the phasing out of NHS beds acted as a further recruiting agent for the private sector. Lee notes that before 1974 independent hospitals gained some 50 to 55 per cent of total private health services expenditure. By 1976 they had cornered 69 per cent of private health service expenditure. 'In the two years from 1974, private health care expenditure in independent hospitals expanded in real terms by about one quarter.'[2]

The key indicator of long-term planning for private health care is to be found in the subscription lists to those organizations covering the cost of private health care. Shortly after the establishment of the NHS, 120,000 persons were insured for private health care, a total which had advanced to over 2 million by 1971. A peak was reached in 1974 when the insured population totalled 2·3 million. The total number insured fell slightly in 1975 and 1976 and this decline 'may well have been linked directly to the uncertainties and controversies of the pay-bed dispute'. It may, too, have been due to the broad economic problem of rapid inflation, rising unemployment and falling real incomes.[3] More recently, the number covered has begun to grow again: up to 2·25 million in 1977, rising to 2·38 million a year later and jumping to 2·76 million in 1979 (a rise of 15·8 per cent).

Important in the renewed growth of private medical insurance has been the role of the company welfare state. We saw earlier in Chapter 8 that companies are increasingly providing medical insurance, not only for their employees but for their employees' families. Even if the employee's family repays the company, companies gain membership at discount rates. Not surprisingly, therefore, demand from company schemes has been increasingly faster than that from individuals themselves. Indeed, while over the period 1966/71 the number of individual subscribers rose by an annual rate of 2·7 per cent, it then fell by a rate of 3·8 per cent in the year up to 1976, falling by 6·5 per cent in 1977 and 3·1 per cent in the following year. This decline has been more than offset by companies taking out private medical insurance for their employees, with a massive rise of 8·6 per cent and 19·1 per cent in 1978 and 1979 respectively. In addition to the boom in company subscriptions the private sector has been recruiting more controversial clients. Reports have appeared of subscriptions taken out for certain police forces[4] and electrical contracting employees.[5] But despite these latest recruits, it is important to recall the information presented in the previous chapter on the company welfare state, which showed that access to private health care is still overwhelmingly limited to high-income earners and their families.

(ii) *Private care in the NHS*

Some private health care is purchased within the National Health Service although this provision has become the

centre of an increasingly bitter political fight over recent
years. Allowing private medicine in the National Health
Service was conceded in the establishment of the NHS.
Aneurin Bevan defended his decision on the grounds that
this was preferable to the development of a separate private
health service and would ensure the cooperation of the
medical profession.

While junior doctors, nurses and other health service
workers were all to be full-time employees of the NHS,
consultants were allowed to choose either to work full-time
for the NHS or to work part-time. Maximum part-timers
receive nine-elevenths of a full-time salary and are allowed
to undertake private practice. Currently, some 43 per cent
of consultants have full-time contracts and 47 per cent
are maximum part-timers. This ratio varies according to
discipline – for example, over 90 per cent of geriatricians
are full-time consultants, while in other areas most consultants are involved in private medicine; almost 90 per
cent of general surgeons, for example, have some private
practice.

While the 1946 Act allowed what are called pay-beds
within the NHS, the Labour Party's October 1974 election
manifesto reaffirmed the party's commitment to 'phase out
private pay-beds from NHS hospitals'. The Health Services Act 1976 provided that 1000 of the 4444 pay-beds
would be phased out by the Secretary of State within six
months, after which the task of phasing out would become
the responsibility of the independent Health Services
Board which would operate under terms laid down by the
Act.

The 1979 Conservative election manifesto made two
promises in respect to the private market in health care.
The first was to allow pay-beds to be provided where there
was a demand for them; the second concerned the restoration of tax relief on employer/employee medical insurance
schemes. The 1980 Health Services Act abolishes the
Health Services Board, ends the enforced withdrawal of
pay-beds from the NHS, introduces amended provisions

for control over private practice and transfers to the Secretary of State the powers of the Board to control the development of private hospitals. So private practice within the NHS continues, at least for the time being.

One of the key objections to allowing this private welfare state to flourish in the NHS is the queue-jumping by those who are able to buy immediate admission, and this charge was considered by the Royal Commission on the NHS. It was reported to the Commission that hospital staff, including junior doctors, nurses and domestic staff, were expected to provide services for private patients outside their normal range of duties without additional pay, and that payment was not always made when hospital equipment and facilities were used for private work. However, the most 'frequent and serious' allegations made to the Commission concerned the speedier admission of private patients, either to pay-beds or, after a private consultation, to NHS beds.

On this charge the Royal Commission noted:

> We have no firm evidence that such abuses are extensive, and we consider that it should be possible to deal with them administratively. Nevertheless, we regard it as important not only that the NHS should be fair to all its patients, but also that it should make every effort to be seen to be fair, and we deplore such 'queue jumping'.

The Commission reported that agreement had been reached between the health departments and medical profession on the introduction of common waiting-lists for urgent and seriously ill NHS and private patients. The Commission welcomed this move, adding that they hoped these arrangements would be extended to all hospital patients.[6]

While private medical insurance does not directly qualify for tax relief, there are a whole series of hidden subsidies from the public purse. The private sector does not have to incur the expense of training its own doctors, nurses and other staff, but relies on those trained in the NHS. Very few of the private hospitals have so far been approved by the General Nursing Council for Training Nurses, and postgraduate medical training takes place exclusively within the NHS. While accepting that pathology and radiology carried out in the NHS for private patients is normally paid for, the Royal Commission on the NHS reported that the availability of such facilities may relieve the private sector of providing what might in some cases be an uneconomic service.[7] These subsidies to private medicine overwhelmingly benefit richer groups. Earlier it was noted that the main boom in private medicine had come from the company sector purchasing subscriptions for their employees. Yet in the company welfare state chapter it was noted that this benefit was bought out of gross income and was restricted to high-income earners and their families. In this way the provision of private medical care helps to widen still further class differences in Britain.

Private welfare state: education

The public schools represent the most conspicuous junction between economic and social privilege. Two considerable advantages follow from them: first, access to Oxbridge; second, access from Oxbridge to positions of political and economic power. In fact, the term 'private education' is misleading. The extent of tax subsidies available to fee-paying parents and to the schools themselves, combined with direct public purchasing of school places, gives them a very large measure of public support.

The fees alone for private education suggest that this is a private market catering for the very top end of the income scale. In fact, as we shall see, they are heavily subsidized while doing so. In 1979, the average annual day-fees stood at £1038 and average boarding fees stood at £2289. By 1980, Eton's fees had risen to £3300 a year while Millfield's had reached £4350. Not surprisingly, therefore, private schools are used overwhelmingly by the social elite of this country. But before looking at the subsidies to private education we first need to look at the numbers using the private market in education and the dividends which arise from this, both in respect to entrance to Oxbridge and the wider job opportunities which follow.

(i) Who gains?

The only comprehensive figure of the social background of fathers of pupils at public schools was reproduced in the report of the Public Schools Commission. This shows that day pupils and, even more so, boarders, were overwhelmingly drawn from parents in social classes 1 and 2. Over eight out of ten pupils at day-schools came from middle- and upper middle-class homes. A similar proportion of children from social classes 1 and 2 occupied boarding-school places, although here one in ten boarding places go to the children of parents in the armed forces.[8]

That one of the advantages of attending a public school is easier access to Oxbridge can be seen in the over-representation of pupils from these schools at Britain's most prestigious universities. First, entrance to Cambridge. While the maintained schools account for 82·2 per cent of the school population, they represent only 47·5 per cent of applications to Cambridge and only 42·4 per cent of those who were accepted came from this sector. On the other hand, independent schools whose pupils make up 10·9 per cent of the school population accounted for 23·1 per cent of applications and 28·5 per cent of the places in 1979. While regulations in 1975 forced direct grant schools to choose between total independence or joining the state system, recent entrance to universities is still classified by whether or not a pupil's school was direct grant. On this basis direct grant school pupils, while amounting to 6·8 per cent of the school-rolls, put in 14·1 per cent of the applications and won 17·1 per cent of the places at Cambridge. Similar figures exist for admissions to Oxford. Students from maintained schools won only 47·3 per cent of the places, while independent and direct grant school pupils gained 35 per cent and 14·6 per cent of places respectively.

While some people might try to argue that pupils from the private sector of education are more intelligent and therefore win more places at Oxbridge, the evidence suggests otherwise. Entrance to Oxbridge has been analysed on the basis of value of 'A'-level scores. The calculations are on the basis of three 'A'-level results and adding together the score for each pass where a grade A scores five points, falling to grade E which scores one point. An examination of the 'A'-level scores of entrants to Cambridge in 1976 shows that those admitted from independent schools had, on average, lower grades than entrants from maintained schools. A similar result is shown when analysing the scores of successful applicants to Oxford University in 1980. If pre-'A'-level candidates are excluded, the proportion of acceptances scoring the highest marks in their 'A'-levels are shown to be pupils from maintained schools. But despite this, only 66 per cent of those with top scores from maintained schools gained entrance to Oxford in 1980, compared with 74 and 72 per cent respectively of top scorers from independent and direct grant schools.

(ii) Top jobs

A place in Britain's private-market educational system not only eases access to Oxbridge but leads to top jobs and completes the circle of privilege. One area which has come under increasing discussion recently is access to top positions in the Civil Service. A report of the House of Commons' Expenditure Committee observed a bias towards Oxbridge graduates, arts graduates and ex-pupils of independent schools in the choice of administrative trainees in the Civil Service. Figures for 1978 show that while 64 per cent of applicants came from maintained schools, this group accounted for only 45 per cent of appointees. In contrast, while only 12 per cent of those who sat the qualifying test came from direct grant schools, pupils from this background made up 21 per cent of administrative trainees appointed in 1978. Similarly, 21 per cent of applicants came from independent schools and they gained up to 29 per cent of offered places as administrative trainees.

The alleged bias towards public school pupils and Oxbridge students was examined by the Civil Service Commission. The Commission reported in the following terms: 'All of us, civil servants and outsiders alike, are satisfied that the discrimination which the Commission exercised in its selection is essentially related to the needs of the job and the qualities required in an administrator in the Civil Service.'[9] This conclusion has been heavily criticized by Robert Maze, a former statistician in the Civil Service Department. Specifically, he has challenged the Commission's findings which explain away any bias in favour of Oxbridge graduates on the grounds that a higher proportion of applicants had first-class degrees and that a higher proportion of Oxbridge graduates generally applied to become administrative trainees.

Robert Maze bases his counter-argument on an analysis of 600 candidates who applied to be administrative trainees in 1975. He found that candidates from Oxbridge and private schools, and men, were given higher Civil Service selection board total marks on written tests than their individual scores and rates seemed to justify. He found even stronger 'unsupported bias' in favour of Oxbridge in the subjective assessments of behaviour. 'These subjective judgements cannot be viewed as valid measures of the candidate; indeed they may well tell us more about the assessors than about the assessed.' Maze added, 'Among candidates of the same ability as measured by every test, exercise and subjective assessment of personality and intellect, those from Oxbridge have a better chance of selection in the final judgement.'[10]

Administrative trainees are viewed as the high-fliers in the Civil Service, and will supply many of tomorrow's senior civil servants. The overlap between use of the private-market educational system and the admission to top jobs can be seen in the summary table below, which shows the heavy concentration of public schoolboys in certain occupations. For example, in 1971 80 per cent of High Court judges and 83 per cent of directors of major insurance companies had been beneficiaries of the private educational system; 78 per cent of members of the Conservative cabinet in 1970 went to public schools compared with 91 per cent in the present administration.

(iii) Who pays?

In one sense public schools are appropriately named, for many of the pupils are heavily subsidized from the Exchequer. The system of subsidies covers tax concessions for parental fees, free or subsidized places from local authorities, the armed forces or the Civil Service, the charitable tax concessions of public schools themselves and a free supply of trained teachers from the state sector. We need to look in a little more detail at each of these subsidies.

The tentacles of the tax welfare state have worked their way into the private market for education. The average fees for boarding school are far more than an unemployed family with a couple of children gain in supplementary benefits in an entire year. Many families using the private market for education send two or three children to public schools. Except for the super-rich, this requires careful funding of school fees to gain the maximum tax conces-

Table 15 *Percentage* of public-school-educated holders of various elite jobs in Britain*

The establishment	
The Civil Service, under-secretary and above (1970)	62
High Court and appeal judges (1971)	80
Church of England bishops (1971)	67
Education	
Vice-chancellors, principals and professors in English and Welsh universities (1967)	33
Heads of colleges and professors at Oxford and Cambridge (1967)	49
Commerce and industry	
Directors of forty major industrial firms (1971)	68
Directors of clearing banks (1971)	80
Directors of major insurance companies (1971)	83
Politics	
Conservative Members of Parliament (1970)	64
Conservative Members of Parliament (1974)	73
Conservative Cabinet (1970)	78
Labour Members of Parliament (1970)	8
Labour Members of Parliament (1974)	9
Labour Cabinet (1970)	29
Base line	
Fourteen-year-olds at school in England and Wales (1967)	2·6

*Percentages rounded. The percentages are the total in each group whose education is known. All public schools are included, but not other independent or direct grant grammar schools.

Source: Ivan Reid, *Social Class Differences in Britain*, Table 6.13.

sions. The main schemes operate in the following ways.

Both capital and income schemes exist to help minimize the cost of school fees. If parents are investing a capital sum, then annuity trust schemes have the advantage in that there is no income tax levied on the money paid out from the trust for school fees; obviously, such a scheme is very attractive to high income taxpayers. Similarly, whether any capital transfer tax is payable when capital is being moved around to pay future school fees partly depends on who gives the money. If payments are made by the parents solely for the maintenance, education or training of their children, such capital payments are free of capital transfer tax either when the money is first invested or when the fees are paid. If the grandparents, or somebody else, give a capital sum for school fees, the money they eventually pay over for school fees will count as gifts for capital transfer tax. However, if the payment from non-parents is made on the basis of an interest-free loan repayable on demand to the grandparents of the child, and the parents invest the money in a trust for the education of their children, there will be no capital transfer tax charge. If the party making the gift writes off the loan at a rate of £2000 a year (or £4000 if both grandparents are involved) the capital gift can be written off over the years without paying capital transfer tax.

If parents are paying for school fees out of current income there are a number of schemes to help meet the fees at minimum cost, but most of them involve the parents taking out a series of investment-type life insurance policies, one of which falls due each year during which the children are at school. We saw earlier how life insurance policies gain a subsidy from the Exchequer, and important as these tax subsidies are, they are small in comparison with the two other major subsidies underpinning this private market welfare state. These are the free places bought for employees by public bodies in the private educational market and, secondly, the subsidies the private sector of education gains by way of charitable status.

(iv) Public's stake

A major subsidy to the private educational system comes from the purchasing of school places by public bodies.

Free or subsidized places can be provided by local authorities. The 1976 Education Act laid down that those local authorities wishing to buy places at independent schools had to obtain the approval of the Secretary of State. This would be granted only on certain conditions; for example, that there was a shortage of suitable places in LEA maintained schools, or a need for denominational education or of boarding-school education. Surprisingly, 80 per cent of applications were approved by the Education Secretary.[11] Since May 1979, however, with a change in the law – one of the first decisions of the incoming Tory government – educational authorities have been free to buy places in the private education market without first seeking the approval of the Education Minister.

The number and cost of these places is considerable. In February 1977 the *Times Educational Supplement* carried a national survey which put LEAs as the purchasers of 40,000 places at independent schools. The estimated cost in 1966/7 was £23 million, although Rick Rogers remarks that the total subsidy from local authorities was well in excess of this sum. Citing figures from the Chartered Institute of Public Finance and Accountancy (CIPFA), Rogers put the total sum at £39·4 million in 1977/8. However, this total excludes the amount local authorities spent in providing special education in the private sector: £47·5 million in the same year. CIPFA estimate the subsidy rising to £85·2 million for non-handicapped pupils' fees in the private sector in 1978/9.

Despite the Labour government's attempts to limit the number of places bought by local authorities, recent figures suggest that the government's objectives were thwarted. Rogers quotes Trafford as an example which, while operating a cash limit of £27,000 for funding non-handicapped, non-denominational pupils at independent schools, was nevertheless able in 1978/9 to secure 1300 denominational and 530 non-denominational places in the private sector. Similarly, Lancashire was listed in a Commons reply as buying 566 places for non-handicapped and

183 places for handicapped pupils in the private sector, yet was funding 2574 places in 1978/9.

These figures will probably show a further increase when the government's Assisted Places scheme comes into operation. The latest statistics show that about 460 of the 1100 schools invited to participate in the scheme have offered 13,000 places. According to this source, 'some of those applying for the highest proportion of assisted places are the thirteen former voluntary-aided grammar schools that went independent, rather than going comprehensive.'[12] The latest estimate of the cost of the Assisted Places scheme shows that the project has been scaled down by about half of the original estimate. Nevertheless, it is proposed that the scheme should begin in 1981 at an initial cost of £3 million and will cater for about 6000 children a year by 1983/4.[13]

A second major consumer of the private educational system is the Ministry of Defence. Ever since 1955, parents working in the armed forces have been eligible for allowances aimed at helping those parents provide 'a continuity of education for their children'. While all ranks are eligible to apply, this subsidy goes overwhelmingly to the highest paid groups in the armed forces, 67 per cent of the allowances being taken up by the officer class. In 1978/9 9030 of the 39,725 male officers took up boarding allowances for their children. While the other ranks made up 263,673, only a fraction over 4000 of them gained an allowance. Rogers puts the cost, including travelling expenses and the cover for claimants' tax liability, at around £23 million. Children from the non-officer class are seen to be the big users of LEA day-schools in this country as well as the British Forces schools abroad.

The third consumer of private education is the diplomatic corps. Children of diplomatic staff are also eligible for boarding-school allowances, as well as travelling fees and day-school fees abroad. In 1978/9 this cost a little in excess of £5 million. Similar arrangements apply to the staff employed in the overseas development administration. Rogers estimates that costs here total £2·7 million. Rogers believes that much of the public data underestimate the true cost of buying these places in the private education market. He cites research by the Campaign for Comprehensive Education which highlighted the failure to cost accurately the fares of children whose fees are paid by the Ministry of Defence, diplomatic staff and overseas development administration. The campaign came up with a minimum estimate in 1978 of £15 million and a maximum of £62·5 million (and the margin is so fantastically wide because public bodies are unwilling to make available the full information). Updating these figures for inflation, Rogers puts the corresponding totals at £18 million and £75 million by 1979.

(v) Charitable gains

The second form of subsidy to the private education market comes by way of charitable status. The tax concessions allowed to private schools follow directly from their charitable status. In the first place, organizations or trusts established for charitable purposes are exempt from income tax, corporation tax and capital gains tax, providing the income or gains concerned are applied to charitable purposes only. In general there are no provisions for income tax relief to a donor for donations made to charities. However, where an individual executes a deed of covenant binding himself to make annual payments to a charity, he can obtain income tax relief for the charity of the tax he has paid on the gift. The same rules apply to companies who execute covenants who obtain corresponding relief from corporation tax.

From 1981/2 onwards, the tax relief allowed to individuals for covenants in favour of charities can be claimed at the higher rates of tax, subject to a ceiling of relief of £3000 per annum, and the time limit over which covenants run has been reduced from over six years to over three years. The exemption from capital transfer tax for transfers to charities on death or within one year of death has also been raised by £200,000. While it is difficult to estimate accurately the tax value of charitable status, the Campaign for Comprehensive Education estimated in 1978 an annual tax loss of £25 million in respect of educational charitable tax concessions. Rogers writes that an unofficial Treasury estimate subsequently indicated that the Campaign for Comprehensive Education's 1978 figure was too low and should have been nearer £30 million. Today it would approach £35 million. Rate relief is estimated currently at £1·2 million.

One of the largest hidden subsidies to the private education market is the training of teachers in the public sector. In June 1977 the average annual cost of training a teacher was put at a little over £2000 in 1976 prices. Given a three-year course, together with inflation, the total cost of training a teacher today would be around £8500. The cost of providing a degree course is put at between £8500 and £10,000. Taking the 40,000 teachers in independent schools, and a breakdown between graduate and non-graduate qualifications, Rogers estimates that the state will have underwritten a cost of training the graduate teachers to the tune of £161·5 million. The majority of private sector teachers have in addition taken training courses. This raises the cost to £170 million if half have so trained and £255 million if three-quarters have obtained this qualification.

In 1970 a research report on the financing of private education estimated that 'direct public support constituted about 20 per cent of the income of the private sector in 1965/6.'[14] Rogers estimates that in 1979 the state was subsidizing the private sector at a rate of a *minimum* of £350 million a year, and at a more likely rate of £500 million-plus. He went on to observe about the private education market that 'it must be the British Leyland of the education world. In 1979, BL received £300 million from the Government and has just been allowed £450

million for 1980, British Steel is to get that much in
1980/1. With its £½ billion plus perhaps the private
education sector should be named British Schools.'

Conclusion

If the distribution of earned income in this country is
unequal, that of unearned income is grossly so, and yet
both sources of income allow an excessive command over
resources by a very privileged elite. Part of their expenditure goes in supporting the fifth welfare state examined
in this book, namely the private market provision of health
and education. The provision of private medical care
through organizations like BUPA continues to grow, and
while individual subscriptions to health insurance companies have been falling, these have been more than offset
by the provisions made by companies for their employees
and their families. The bulk buying of insurance by companies results in employees picking up this advantage at
a cut-price level. Moreover, the company's subscription
for its employees is set against taxable income – so
reducing the tax base still further. As well as the hidden
contributions from the Exchequer, all of which widen
rather than diminish inequality, there is some evidence to
show that the NHS subsidizes the private sector.

Similar subsidies from the state sector are given to the
private sector of education: both central and local government buy a considerable number of places in the major
private schools; the overwhelming majority of teachers in
these schools are trained in the state sector; and the schools
themselves attract charitable status. On top of this, the tax
benefit welfare state operates in a way to help minimize
the cost of fees for those parents who are involved directly
in meeting the education bills for their children. Such tax
concessions not only reduce the price of buying into the

private sector of education but push up the burden of taxation for other taxpayers. Moreover, expenditure in buying places in the private market produces its first dividend by gaining easier access to Oxbridge, and from there to top elite positions in industry, commerce and the Civil Service. Reform of the private market welfare state can only be sensibly pursued within a comprehensive policy embracing all five welfare states. This is the subject-matter of the following chapter.

11. Freedom First: a Programme of Reform

Before we start to outline a total programme of reform of Britain's five welfare states, it is important to recall the main principles from which the reforms stem. The overriding aim is to increase the freedom of large sections of the community by eradicating poverty. Only by reforming all five welfare states will the resources be available to restructure the additional benefit welfare state so that it provides a minimum floor on which people can build by their own efforts. We have shown how poverty affects *large* numbers of people – though at different periods of their lives – and to prevent this poverty the reforms will need to bring about a four-fold cash redistribution: from rich to poor, state to individual, from men to women and from the more affluent to the least affluent periods of each person's life.

The first item on the agenda is the reform of the traditional welfare state. Seven constituent reforms are detailed and it is proposed that they should be implemented in stages as the money becomes available from the tax reforms outlined in the second half of the chapter (Appendix I details the costs of the reforms). The first key change is the implementation of a full child benefit scheme while the second is the scrapping of the contribution conditions for national insurance benefits and the restructuring of the National Insurance Fund into a social security budget. The third reform is the introduction of a more generous unemployment benefit. The fourth reform introduces a new one-parent family allowance, and the fifth proposal is to extend eligibility for benefits to all disabled people. The sixth reform is the introduction of a pensioner tax credit, and the last stage of the reform programme is the inclusion of average rent payments with national insurance benefits.

Reform

(i) Child benefit

There is a whole bevy of reasons why a major increase in child benefit is a prerequisite of all the other welfare reforms. First, an overall reform of the traditional welfare state without significantly increasing the level of child benefit is likely to undermine public support for the programme. The reason for this is simple. In the 1920s, when unemployment benefit was cut in real terms, additional payments for children for the unemployed were made in an attempt to stave off widespread political unrest. From that day since, the payments for the children of the unemployed have been more generous than the support given to working families with children. The result is that while only in a small number of instances (the numbers are much exaggerated) are families better off on the dole, many more working families find themselves only marginally better off when in work.[1] Any welfare reform programme which fails to equalize the payments for children irrespective of whether their parents are working or not will run the risk of bringing the whole of the traditional welfare system into greater disrepute. Failure to act on child benefits will therefore continue to place the working poor at a disadvantage to the poor who are unable to work. Such a situation offends a widespread feeling about fairness in our society, and encourages political capital to be made out of those who, for reasons beyond their control, are better off out of work.

Second, while many old people are enveloped in poverty

as soon as they retire, to a greater and greater extent poverty is wearing a young face. An increase in child benefit is the most immediate and effective means of tackling the problem of family poverty among those who work, and it does so in a way which increases the incentive to work rather than the reverse. Child benefits at present are paid to all families but are deducted from any other social security payments for children. The larger the child benefit, therefore, the greater the difference in income between a family when it is in work and when it is dependent on benefit.

Third, child benefit changes are also important as a means of maintaining tax equity. Since 1909, when child tax allowances were re-introduced, Chancellors could maintain tax equity between childless taxpayers and those with children by increasing child tax allowances at the same time as other personal allowances were revised. 1977 saw the phasing out of child tax allowances to coincide with the introduction of child benefits. With the final abolition of child tax allowances in April 1980 (except for taxpayers with dependent children overseas), child benefits took on a dual function. On the one hand they are the most effective way of channelling resources to families on low income. On the other hand they are the only mechanism by which Chancellors can increase the tax-free income of taxpayers with children when making regular revisions of the tax threshold for other taxpayers. Chapter 6 detailed how the tax burden has moved against not only the low paid but also households with children. The introduction of a generous system of child benefits will play an important part in redressing this horizontal inequity in the tax system.

Fourth, a generous system of child benefits will play a crucial part in transforming the welfare state into a system of benefits on which people can build by their own efforts and not be penalized for doing so. Child benefits at the present time are tax-free. They are kept in total by families in work, irrespective of the family's level of earnings. Any programme, and particularly one which will be immensely expensive, will have to be implemented in stages. A big increase in child benefits will have an immediate and important effect on the activities of those families living on incomes near to the poverty line. For example, the ideal way of tackling poverty among single-parent families is the introduction of a single-parent family allowance (and this is advocated later). Yet the doubling of child benefits in real terms would bring about a significant reduction in the number of one-parents dependent on means-tested supplementary benefits. Some would have their incomes taken above the supplementary benefit poverty line and therefore become ineligible. But other one-parent families, whose income was not brought up to the poverty line, might well decide that child benefit payments now provided enough of a launching-pad to free themselves from means-tested benefit support, providing this was accompanied by the provision of adequate day-care facilities for their children.[2]

There is one other major advantage which will stem from concentrating the first effort on child benefit. The advent of adequate child benefit payments will increase the economic power and status of women in our society. As we have seen, family poverty among the working poor is characteristic of households with young children. Many families are sprung from poverty only by a second wage in the household. But, despite the poverty which it entails, many mothers prefer to remain at home when their children are very young. Adequate child benefits will increase their income as of right and should be linked with the introduction of a home responsibility allowance (for which people caring for aged relatives will also be eligible), financed by the phasing out of the married man's tax allowance.

At the present time, over £7 million is lost in revenue by the married man's tax allowance. As we saw in Chapter 6, the group which has suffered least from the increasing burden of taxation in the post-war period has been the two-wage-earning childless households. The choice before married women, under the proposed reforms, would be to continue receiving this tax subsidy throughout the working lives of their husbands, or for this subsidy to be concentrated in a cash payment during those years when women are most vulnerable, i.e., when they have very young children. To accompany the changes in child benefits, the government should be seeking the views of taxpayers on the desirability of freezing the married man's tax allowance so as to finance the introduction of the mother's allowance.

The one group which would be put at the greatest disadvantage by such a move is those middle- to late-middle-age two-wage-earning households. But they, together with single taxpayers living in somebody else's household, are the relatively affluent groups at each band of income. Moreover, the proposal is not to cancel the married man's tax allowance but rather to freeze it at its present level. Put in the broadest terms, a switch from the married man's allowance, which represents the dependent status of women, to a mother's allowance, combined with a generous child benefit, would confirm and extend the social status and economic choice of women.

This brings us on to the question of the level to which child benefit should be raised. Indeed, there is the general question about the relative level of all benefits. Other countries have produced standards-of-living budgets, and while it is desirable that similar studies be undertaken in this country, we know from other work (Chapter 2) that the children's rates are low in relation to the adult rates, and that the life afforded on the ordinary supplementary benefit level is insufficient to prevent real hardship for anybody dependent upon it for a long period of time. It is important, therefore, for all claimants who are on benefit for any length of time to have an income at the long-term national insurance benefit level. When budgetary studies have been concluded, and the resources are available, adjustments to the current relativities can be made, including to the rates for children.

At the present time, the national insurance system pays

allowances for children at two levels. The lower level is paid to the children whose parents are sick or unemployed. At the present time, these allowances, together with child benefit, come to £6 a week. A higher allowance of £12.25, including child benefits, is paid to children whose parents are drawing what are called the higher national insurance benefits such as invalidity, widows', widowed mothers' and retirement pensions. As a first stage, child benefits need to be raised to equal the total payments made to the children of unemployed and sick claimants. A second stage would involve their being raised to the £12.25 level.[3]

The achievement of a generous system of child benefits, together with the beginnings of a mother's allowance, would not only eradicate family poverty as we know it today, but would also increase in a very real sense the economic freedom of many households with children. It would be a practical recognition of the importance of the work done by mothers and would support her responsibility for raising a family. It would also begin to disengage families from the means-tested welfare state and, because child benefit provides a floor, add significantly to the freedom of poorer families to live their lives as they choose rather than within the guidelines laid down by regulations.

There is also a need to accompany the changes in child benefits with an examination of whether they need to be accompanied by the introduction of a statutory minimum wage. Seebohm Rowntree was clear on the need to operate both policies at once when he commented on the original Beveridge proposals. Rowntree went back to his 1936 data and reworked the income schedules, taking into account the full implementation of the Beveridge plan. We know that the plan was not fully implemented, but even so, on the assumption of full implementation, Rowntree found that 7 per cent of the working-class population of York would still have been in poverty, and he added: 'York is not a low-wage city and I have no reason to suppose that figures in other towns would on average have shown more favourable results.' Rowntree then went on to argue: 'If that be so then it is clear that if *all* involuntary poverty is to be abolished we need not only the Beveridge plan but also a statutory minimum wage.' Rowntree accepted that a minimum wage would be of some benefit to casual labourers, though just how much would depend on the number of hours they worked. It would also be of considerable help to childless workers who may not be in the greatest need. However, he insisted: 'The fact that the Beveridge plan will not lead to the abolition of the large amount of poverty due to inadequate earnings is no reflection on the plan – it was not designed to do so,' adding that this argument leads 'quite clearly to the need for a national minimum wage'.[4]

An obvious first step along this road would be a more rigorous policy of enforcing the legal minimum wages laid down by wages councils. A second move would be an examination of the effect a minimum wage has in each of the countries in which it now operates, both on the relative rewards of the low paid (have differentials re-established themselves after a short period of time?) and on the employment levels of lower paid workers.

(ii) New social security tax

As we have seen earlier (Chapter 5), most of the major non-means-tested benefits are paid from the National Insurance Fund. The financing aspect of the welfare state was shown to be highly regressive, poorer workers paying a much higher percentage of their income in national insurance contributions than the very highest paid. This side of the Beveridge scheme was attacked by Aneurin Bevan for, as his biographer tells us, 'Like many other Socialists he had always been reluctant to agree to basing social services on insurance schemes, holding that the non-contributory principle could have the double advantage of avoiding unnecessary bureaucracy and a poll tax masqueraded as an insurance premium.'[5] Bevan was not alone in his criticism. The PEP and the Association of Approved

Societies argued with Beveridge that his scheme should be one of flat-rate benefits in return for graduated contributions.

Against these criticisms, and the strong argument marshalled by James Meade on financing benefits by a surcharge on income tax, Beveridge was only too pleased to side with Keynes who argued that the national insurance principle was a useful 'fiction', both for making employers share the costs of welfare and for dispelling popular myths that the Exchequer had a bottomless purse.[6]

The more important factor in clinching the argument, however, was Beveridge's belief that the insurance principle was in keeping with the wishes of most working-class people. It is impossible to do justice to Beveridge's view without taking into account the role of means-testing in the life of many working-class families in the 1920s and 1930s and of their deep hatred of this system. The idea of an insurance-based welfare state giving rights of citizenship had, in T. H. Marshall's words, overwhelming appeal, and the mutual responsibility implied in the social contract of national insurance remains compelling. In addition, the trade unions argued that an insurance fund would prevent governments cutting the level of benefits, particularly the dole.

This argument still has an appeal in Labour circles when proposals for reforming the welfare state are discussed. For example, in its most important document on reforming the welfare state issued since Beveridge, the Labour party observed:

> there is a legitimate fear among trade unionists that if the state took over the whole responsibility for financing social benefits, then the state might one day slash those benefits in order to weather an economic storm. As long as the benefits are 'earned' by payment of contributions and are financed out of an insurance fund, they are felt to be something which the worker receives as of right and which no politician can take away from him.[7]

This argument is, however, rather confused. It is a strange form of logic which talks of the state taking over the whole responsibility for financing social security benefits. The state has no money by itself, but only those funds raised in taxation and by other means. If one drops the word 'state' in the above quotation and substitutes 'taxpayer' or 'worker', then the silliness of this position is clearly exposed. Moreover, as that perceptive critic, Kathleen Hood, commented, history suggests that a National Insurance Fund is not a bulwark against benefits being cut. 'The fact that the workers had contributed to Unemployment Insurance did not prevent the government from slashing those benefits in 1931 – moreover the case for doing so was ... partly argued on the grounds that we must return to the "insurance principle".'[8] And, as we commented upon in Chapter 5, in the 1950s, when the National Insurance Fund was showing a very healthy surplus, pensions and other benefits were not increased. Instead, the government decided to halve the Exchequer contribution to the Fund. More recently the insurance principle has not prevented Margaret Thatcher from cutting unemployment benefit in real terms for the first time since the 1930s.

We have seen that Keynes argued that the national insurance principle was a useful fiction and one to be encouraged as a means of chivvying out of workers and employers funds for the welfare state. But legislators have taken the fiction seriously when laying down the eligibility conditions for benefits. If a scheme is based on the insurance principle, benefits are limited to those who have paid adequate contributions. So, in Arthur Marwick's words: 'Along with the insurance principle went a whole wilderness of qualifications and requalification conditions and limits upon the length of time for which benefits would be paid.'[9]

At the present time, information about claimants not receiving benefit because they fail to satisfy contribution conditions is available only for sickness and unemployment benefit, and the estimates for these benefits are 35,900 and 178,000 claimants respectively.[10] A much larger number of claimants – e.g., a third of a million pensioners – receive benefit at a reduced amount because of an incomplete contribution record, while a third of a million claimants have exhausted their right to benefit.[11] But it is important to remember that these are snapshots giving totals at one point of time only. They do not record the total number affected in a year – let alone in a lifetime.

The one major advantage we now have in the 1980s, resulting from politicians pushing the insurance principle for forty or more years, is that people understand that they have earned the right to the major non-means-tested benefits. This belief is part of our political culture. To move away from the poll-tax financing of the National Insurance Fund to a social security tax would not therefore evoke fears among the electorate that one was returning to a means-tested welfare state. In fact, the reverse would l e true. At the same time, the reform would have the added advantages of simplifying the qualification rules for benefit and making the financing of the welfare state itself an agent of redistribution (in addition to the redistributionary elements in the payment of benefits themselves).

It is important that the new benefits continue to be called insurance benefits, but the eligibility rules must be over-hauled. Since an important part of the welfare state is paid direct from the Exchequer, and since funds come from both direct and indirect taxation, people will be 'earning' their right to benefit even if they are not in work and paying the national insurance contributions. For British-born subjects, the right to national insurance benefits should be granted as soon as need arises. There is no difficulty, either, in granting benefit to those foreign nationals working in this country where there is a reciprocal arrangement with their country (as there is in the EEC). A much more difficult question is how to treat the right to benefit of other foreign nationals, and this question needs a careful and full public debate.

As well as radically loosening the eligibility rules for national insurance benefits, it is also proposed that a major overhaul be made of the method of contribution. The National Insurance Fund should be abolished and replaced by a social security and health budget which would have three main sources of income. There would be contributions from employers and from employees and a general contribution from the Exchequer. The employers' contribution should continue along the present lines with one change: the ceiling on contributions should be abolished so that the present proportional employers' tax should continue, but be paid on all incomes no matter how high. The employees' contribution will be abolished. The equivalent revenue will be raised by levelling a social security tax paid in addition to income tax. At the present time, employee contributions raise £4859 millions. The same sum could be raised by adding 7 pence on to the standard rate of income tax. In addition, it is important to maintain an Exchequer contribution to the Fund so that the 'rights' to benefits of those not in work are safeguarded. A second reform in the contributions can occur when the income-tax changes proposed later in this chapter are brought into effect. A graduated surcharge can then be levied on each of the different bands of income, with a smaller surcharge on each of the lower bands of income tax.

(iii) A new unemployment benefit

The next task is the introduction of new benefits or the major revamping of existing benefits. Here it is important to make a distinction between claimants who are over retirement age and those who are not. In examining claimants below retirement age, those in greatest and most persistent need are to be found among the unemployed and single-parent families.

The majority of politicians argue that the most effective

way of helping the unemployed is to provide jobs, but, sadly, full employment does not look to be a realistic target in the immediate future and benefits for the unemployed are therefore of key importance. Since 1966 the unemployed may be eligible for a flat-rate benefit for up to twelve months and an earnings related benefit for the first six months of unemployment. Notwithstanding the rise in unemployment over the past few years, the Thatcher government is planning to phase out earnings-related supplements which are paid for the first six months of unemployment[12] even though the supplements have been effective in keeping large numbers of people off means-tested assistance. But because the scheme did favour higher paid workers, and the payments were made during that period when families were most likely to have more adequate resources, the reforms outlined here do not envisage the re-introduction of earnings-related supplements. Rather, the plan is for a flat-rate benefit for the first twelve months of unemployment, at the end of which claimants would be eligible for the higher national insurance benefit rates.

Changes in the eligibility rules and in the value of unemployment benefit should be tied in with the government's retraining programme so that claimants' skills are developed to match the changing needs of the economy. The government's job centres and retraining programmes must be linked to the system of paying unemployment benefit, and benefit should be payable only so long as suitable jobs have not been refused without good cause, or claimants have refused, without good cause, to undertake retraining programmes.

(iv) A one-parent-family allowance

Until the recent record increase in the numbers of unemployed, the fastest growing group of poor people were single parents and their children. Indeed, the information in Chapter 3 shows that the largest single group of claimants below retirement age dependent on means-tested supplementary benefit are single-parent families. Only when the dependants are included in the total do we find that the unemployed drawing supplementary benefit are the larger group.

The introduction of a generous system of child benefits will not only have an immediate effect on the livelihood and aspirations of many single-parent families, but will also make the introduction of a single-parent-family allowance much more politically acceptable. Most of the discussion up until now about a non-means-tested benefit for single-parent families has been built on the assumption of an inadequate system of child support. The result was the formulation of policies which suggested the payment of generous benefits to the mother (or father) so as to cover her and her children's needs. But while there is widespread sympathy for the children of single parents, such goodwill does not extend to all single parents themselves who are often seen as the authors of their own problems. This may be unfair and unjust but it is an awkward fact of life. A single-parent-family allowance based on the mother maximized all the difficult questions about policing the benefit to prevent abuse, and never gave an adequate answer to the charge that such a scheme could put the wife of a low-wage earner at an unfair disadvantage to the single parent.

As well as gaining all the advantages outlined earlier, a generous system of child benefit unties this Gordian knot. The children of single-parent families will be treated equally with other children. The more generous the level of child benefit going to all children, the lower will be the proportion of the single-parent-family's income coming from a non-means-tested single-parent-family allowance. Similarly, the more generous the new home-responsibility allowance, the smaller the proportion of one-parent-family's income will be made up for the new allowance.

The proposal is for a one-parent-family allowance to be introduced only after the full implementation of the child benefit payments. The discussion is therefore about at what level this allowance should be set, and it is proposed to introduce the allowance in two stages. The first is to pay the single parent's allowance at the non-contributory invalidity benefit level; the second is to bring this level up to the high rate paid for widows. However, there are social and political difficulties in introducing both stages of this reform and they need to be faced squarely. The cause of one-parent families is not advanced by pretending that no difficulties exist, particularly over the co-habitation rule.

This rule operates in order to maintain equity between the wife of a low-wage earner (who cannot claim supplementary benefits, and who obviously will not be eligible for a single-parent-family allowance) and the single-parent family on benefit. Its purpose is to prevent the payment of benefits to women who have husbands in all but name. For obvious reasons, the co-habitation rule is bitterly resented by one-parent families. At the moment it is a difficult rule to operate and in 1977 29 per cent of cases where benefit was withdrawn due to suspected co-habitation were reversed during the appeal process.

Three reforms are therefore advocated. In the first place, the rules about what constitutes a one-parent family must be set out clearly in the published regulations to the new benefit. As Paul Lewis has written: 'If other subtle human behaviour patterns such as cruelty or intent can be defined so can co-habitation.'[13] Second, those claiming the single-parent-family allowance will be asked to sign a statement that they are a single-parent family – just as the unemployed have to sign on for benefit and the sick produce medical evidence. Policing the new benefit will therefore remain, and this issue should not be dodged. However, the claimant's position will be much strengthened in that what constitutes co-habitation will have been defined and made public. Moreover, one-parent families will benefit by the third reform. This is that the single-parent allowance for the parent will continue for a set period of time once the circumstances of the one-parent family have changed. In other words, the aim is to allow those one-parent families who wish to become two-parent families to do so. The one-parent family needs a guarantee of their own income of right at the beginnings of a new relationship. Moreover, as all the welfare reforms are prefaced by the introduction of a generous system of child benefits, no new father (the vast majority of single parents are mothers) will be asked to contribute excessively towards the keep of another man's children.

(v) A new disability benefit

The bewildering variety of help available to the disabled has been well illustrated in the work of the Disability Alliance,[14] and in order to bring a greater degree of fairness into the current system it is necessary to distinguish between the two broad requirements of the disabled both of which entail compensation payments. The first is for loss of earnings and the second is to cover the cost of disability. Currently there are three compensation payments for loss of earnings: industrial injuries payment, invalidity benefit and the non-contributory invalidity benefit. The most valuable is the industrial injury benefit which pays the claimant an injury-related allowance on top of the invalidity benefit. The next most valuable payment is the invalidity benefit which is paid to disabled claimants who, after they have received sickness benefit for six months, still remain unfit for work. Others who are disabled – sometimes from birth – may qualify for the non-contributory invalidity benefit (NCIP) from the age of sixteen (or over nineteen if still at school or full-time college) but the value of the benefit is below the national insurance rates for the sick and the unemployed, and well below the contributory invalidity benefit rate.

The reforms already proposed will be of considerable help for the disabled, particularly the major revision of the contributory basis for benefit. This revision will allow the

NCIP to be used as the entrance into the invalidity benefit scheme. Claimants could serve a six-month probationary period on the NCIP (as do others claiming sickness benefit) before becoming eligible for invalidity benefit.

A second stage in reforming the traditional benefit welfare rate for the disabled will centre on the introduction of some kind of disabled allowance, and while the outline of the scheme can be sketched in, this is an issue which requires some more careful consideration. The allowance should be paid to compensate people for the degree to which their disability restricts them from ordinary activities. The suggestion of the Disability Alliance is that this benefit should be paid only after six months of sickness/disability and if there is no early prospect of recovery. The Alliance further suggests that there should be provisional and long-term allowances depending on the expectations of an assessment board about the long-term nature of the degree of disablement. As with war and industrial injury disablement pensions, the disablement allowance should be payable whether or not those eligible receive retirement pensions or other social security benefits. It would not be set against other forms of income, but like all social security benefits (apart from child benefits in the initial stages) it should be liable to tax.

The introduction of a disablement allowance should build on the existing arrangements which already go some way in compensating people for the extra costs of disability. The mobility allowance is paid to disabled people aged between five years and retirement age if they are unable to walk. Some disabled people qualify for the attendance allowance. This is paid at two levels depending on the degree of disability. The benefit is, as its name suggests, paid to a claimant to help over the costs of attending to him; the higher rate, which covers attendance both day and night, is called the constant attendance allowance. In addition, a person other than the disabled claimant may be eligible for an invalid care allowance if they are of working age, provide more than thirty-five hours of care a week, and the disabled person is in receipt of the attendance or constant attendance allowance.

(*vi*) *Pensioner credits*

There are a number of reasons why pension reforms have been kept separate from those already discussed. While it is true to say that many people become poor when they retire, a large number of pensioners are not poor in the way poverty has been defined in this book, because of the extent of their savings or membership of an occupational pension scheme. Moreover, because a large proportion of pensioners are not poor, any increase in their national insurance benefits is not only immensely expensive, but results in a considerable proportion of extra resources going to households with income above the poverty line. This is, of course, true of all the other reforms advocated here, but with one important difference. A higher proportion of the unemployed, sick, disabled and one-parent families are poor compared to pensioners and these groups are also more likely to have family responsibilities.

A second, and more important reason for considering pensioners as a separate group when reforming the traditional benefit welfare state is that since the late 1950s numerous schemes have been put forward to transform radically the structure of state pensions. All but one of these proposals have floundered, either because of political ineptitude, timing, or perhaps because the schemes themselves were so complicated that it was impossible to present them in a way that would enthuse the electorate. The attempt by the last Labour government to win a bipartisan approach to pension reforms was, however, successful and, as a result, the 1975 Pension Act was passed. The main provisions of the reform ensure that each contributor receives a basic pension. This will represent £1 a week for every £1 of a person's earnings up to that basic level (which is revised each year) and a quarter of a worker's earnings between the basic minimum level and an upper limit (set at seven times the basic minimum). The pension gained on the earnings above the basic level is known as the additional pension.

The pension scheme is weighted to favour those on lower incomes and, had the scheme been fully operative by 1975, a single person whose weekly earnings had been £20 would have received on retirement a pension valued at 68 per cent of earnings. The pension is calculated on a worker's best twenty years of earnings so as to help those who have low earnings early in their career, those whose earnings have passed their peak by the time they retire, and women who have to leave their jobs for a while to look after a family. All workers are covered by the scheme unless they are contracted-out, and while full pensions will not be paid until the scheme has been running for twenty years, additional pensions are already being paid.

This is an important point to remember when thinking about a reform of the traditional benefit welfare state. If, as seems likely, the present parliament runs its full length and Labour wins the next election, a Labour government will take office at a time when we have almost reached the mid-point in building up full contributions to the new pension scheme and, as each year passes, the value of the additional pensions in payment increases. Unlike all other groups in poverty which we have so far considered, tomorrow's pensioners already have a measure on the statute book which will in turn raise their relative income and, for the first time, break the link between poverty and old age.

We therefore need to consider ways by which the existing provisions can be supplemented to help today's poor pensioners. One possible measure is the introduction of a pensioner tax credit. In the early 1970s the Heath government published a Green Paper on tax credits. The Green Paper was correctly hailed as the most radical set of welfare proposals to see the light of day since the publication of the Beveridge Report, but it attracted considerable criticism, particularly from poverty groups who argued that, given the cost of introducing a tax credit scheme, the money could be spent more effectively in helping the poor. These were not criticisms which I fully endorsed. Any scheme which introduces universal benefits, or credits, will usually give more help collectively to those above the poverty line than those below.

It is unlikely that the present Conservative government will introduce a tax credit scheme. There are a number of reasons for this. First and foremost are the technical difficulties associated with the slow progress in computerizing the Inland Revenue. Until the Revenue is computerized, the introduction of a total tax credit scheme is severely limited. I would also hazard a guess that there is another stumbling block in the way of this present Conservative government's introducing a comprehensive tax credit scheme, even if the machinery were there to implement it. Tax credits were proposed by the Heath government and there is considerable resistance by the present regime to view any aspect of the Heath government with sympathy, let alone with favour.

These political obstacles need not prevent the Labour Party from looking at the feasibility of implementing a second stage of the tax credit proposals. Child benefits gave birth in all but name to the child tax credit side of the scheme. A second raid into the tax credit proposals could be achieved by hiving off the pensioner tax credit. And, again, time may well be on the side of a future Labour government. Currently, the government are making decisions on the computerization of the PAYE system. Once a decision has been made, it will take at least four years for the scheme to come into full operation. Four years hence will take us into the next parliament and therefore offer an opportunity for an incoming government to implement part of the tax credit proposals if it so wished.

How effective this would be in lifting pensioners off supplementary benefit and rent and rate rebates would depend first on the size of the credit and secondly on the speed at which the proposals for a rent addition to national insurance benefits were introduced. At a recent Civil Service seminar on reforming the welfare state it was suggested that an injection of £600 million into a pensioner tax credit would float 1 million people off supplementary benefits, although on the present rules many, if not most, of those would still be in receipt of rent or rate rebates. Even so, it does seem that the introduction of a pensioner tax credit is worth serious consideration. Any monies paid into the scheme will be for a limited period of time, and will decline in value as the 1975 Pension Act slowly comes into operation.

(vii) Rent allowances

The seventh proposal for reforming the traditional benefit welfare state is that consideration be given to the payment of a rent addition to householders drawing national insurance benefits.

In the section on the failure of the Beveridge plan (Chapter 4) we quoted Seebohm Rowntree's observation that the reforms would not abolish poverty because of their failure to meet in full a claimant's rent or housing costs. Recently, there have been a number of proposals for reform on this front including a means-tested one from David Donnison, who until recently was the chairman of the Supplementary Benefits Commission.[15] Other reformers have emphasized the need for a universal approach,[16] and a less sophisticated non-means-tested approach would be to add on to the householder rate of each of the national insurance benefits an allowance equal to the average rent payments of supplementary benefit claimants.

One reason why this reform is considered here, at the end of the list, is not only because it will be costly, but its importance will be reduced as the other reforms are brought into effect. Unfortunately the government has been unable to provide any estimates on the numbers which would be freed from supplementary benefits as each of the above reforms take effect. Only as the programme was being completed would we be able to see how important the payment of a rent allowance is in raising the income of claimants above the supplementary benefit poverty line.

Tax reforms

This radical rebuilding of the traditional benefit welfare state will be costly but these costs will be met by redistributing resources from the other four welfare states. The remainder of the chapter examines five major tax reforms. The scrapping of the national insurance poll tax is only one part of the reform of our direct system of taxation. Reform of the direct system of taxation needs to be carried out while at the same time limiting the growth of expenditures in the four other welfare states.

The personal allowances play two roles in the tax system: they exempt a certain level of income from tax and they also build a gradation into the whole direct system of taxation. We have already seen that the tax threshold is below the supplementary benefit poverty line and this is particularly so for taxpayers with children. While one way of raising the tax threshold is to increase the personal allowances, such a move has two major disadvantages. In the first place, any increase in the personal allowances cannot distinguish between those with children and those without. It is therefore a very indiscriminate way of raising the tax threshold for taxpayers with young dependants. But there is a second disadvantage entailed with operating on the personal allowances, which is that an increase in the allowances not only helps those at the bottom of the income pile, but all other taxpayers as well. Moreover, as we have seen, the larger a person's income the greater the value these personal allowances are, as they reduce a taxpayer's marginal rate of tax.

The most effective way of raising the tax-free income of taxpayers with children is to increase child benefits. This move has already been advocated as the first priority in reforming the welfare benefit state and it is also the number one priority for changes in the tax system. In addition, four other policies need to be pursued in order to achieve a comprehensive overhauling of the direct system of taxation in this country.

(i) Tax allowances at standard rate only

Chapter 7 gave details of how the tax allowance welfare state worked in favour of those on higher incomes. Not only do those higher up in the income scale have the ability to capitalize from the whole tax benefit welfare state, but, ironically, the higher the income of the taxpayer the greater is the value of each of the tax allowances. Way back in 1975 I first proposed an immediate reform of the tax benefit welfare state whereby tax allowances would in future be allowed only at the standard rate of tax. This reform would leave the tax benefit welfare state intact, but as the benefits could only be claimed at whatever the standard rate of tax is, the value of benefits would be uniform rather than favouring the rich as they do at the moment. Since then, this proposal has met with widespread support and should be acted upon as the first stage of implementing these reforms.

(ii) Cash ceiling on tax benefits

The second reform entails the placing of cash ceilings on all but the personal tax allowances. Since the Labour government first began to operate cash ceilings on the traditional welfare state, we have slowly become aware of how effective this policy is for curtailing public expenditure. A similar policy should be operated on each of the non-personal tax benefits including mortgage interest and life assurance relief.

The need for such a policy is obvious when we look at how expenditure has grown in just one area of the tax benefit welfare state, compared with the traditional welfare state. If expenditure on social security is revalued at constant prices, and a similar exercise is carried out for the tax benefit paid in mortgage interest relief, we find an expenditure of £5918 million on social security in 1960/1 and £286 million in mortgage interest relief. By 1978/9 these totals stood at £15,441 million and £1621 million respectively. Over this period, therefore, the increase in social security expenditure at constant prices was in the order of 61 per cent whereas the tax benefit paid by way of mortgage interest relief rose by 82 per cent.

The difference in the size of the increase on both benefits cannot be explained away by arguing that the 1960/1 data take a fairly high expenditure for social security benefits and a relatively low one for the mortgage interest tax benefit – thereby giving a greater percentage increase to the expenditure on mortgage interest relief. If a later date is taken – 1968/9 – we find an expenditure on social security benefits in constant 1978/9 prices of £10,061 million compared with £594 million in mortgage interest tax relief. Over the following ten years, the increase in social security benefits measured in constant prices is a little less than 35 per cent compared with an over 63 per cent increase in the expenditure on mortgage interest relief. Moreover, as we have seen, the tax relief on mortgage interest is only one of three subsidies to the owner-occupier.

A policy of cash ceilings on the tax benefit welfare state will work in the following way. The proposal is that the current expenditure of these reliefs should be taken as a cash ceiling. In other words, if this policy was operating in 1979/80, a cash ceiling of £1·4 billion would be put on financing the tax benefits for mortgage interest relief. The building societies would be told that this was the total sum available and that they should share this equally among those taxpayers who are at present claiming mortgage interest tax relief. Already a policy of operating the reliefs at the standard rate will be in operation, hence simplifying the administration of the new scheme by the building societies. The societies will have to estimate the numbers of net additional borrowers each year and how the tax benefit is to be spread among them. Currently, the building societies operate a standard deduction scheme for savers whereby the societies automatically deduct and pay the standard rate of tax to the government on interest accruing to each of their savers. A cash ceilings limit on the tax benefit welfare state will be operating a not too dissimilar policy in reverse. Paying each mortgagee the same sum would not only be an equalitarian measure but one which would also be easiest to operate. However, considerable pressure would be applied to link the size of the rebates to mirror the size of the mortgage.

(iii) Paying for company welfare

The third reform is to limit the growing expenditure on company welfare. In common with all the welfare states except the benefit welfare state, company welfare increases rather than diminishes inequality by benefiting most those on high income. At the present time, company welfare expenditure is deducted from a company's gross income and thereby reduces its tax liability. Some monies which would otherwise go to the Exchequer are redirected into the pockets of employees, particularly higher paid employees. There is therefore a case for saying that such expenditure should be made from the company's income after tax has been paid. In a free society companies must be allowed to develop the company welfare state, but not with the present help they gain from the Exchequer. In addition, the 'income' derived from such benefits must be valued accurately and brought within the tax net.

(iv) An exemption scheme

The fourth suggested reform is one which will take longer to implement and will need a further discussion. It is to revert back to the exemption scheme which operated in the income tax system up to 1920 and the outlines of which were given in *To Him Who Hath*.[17] Here it is only necessary to sketch in the broad outlines of the reform.

The proposal is that the personal allowances should be replaced by a specific exemption limit. The exemption limit would ensure that incomes below this level were excluded from tax altogether, but those who earn more than the limit will be assessed for tax on each £1 they earn. However, the reform cannot be one of reverting simply to the pre-1920 scheme. The problem with a specific exemption expressed as a maximum level of income beyond which an individual's income becomes taxable is that it carries with it a dramatically high marginal rate of tax as income moves above the exemption limit. For example, if the exemption limit is put at £x, then as a taxpayer's income moves to £x plus £1 the whole of his income becomes liable to tax. One way of overcoming this drawback is to introduce a vanishing exemption which diminishes in value as income rises but is not withdrawn abruptly at any single crossover point. Such a system would ensure a smooth withdrawal of the exemption as income rises while at the same time ensuring that taxpayers were not faced with a large jump in their marginal rates of tax.

To Him Who Hath gave the following notional figures for such a vanishing exemption scheme. It was suggested that income up to, say, a maximum of £1000 could qualify for 100 per cent exemption. On incomes above this level, however, the value of exemption would be reduced by a third of the difference between gross income and the maximum exemption of £1000. At £2000, therefore, the exemption would be at two-thirds the full rate (£666·66) and at £3000 the exemption would be at a third of the £1000 exemption limit. On this model the exemption would be totally lost at incomes of £4000 and above.

It must be stressed that these are only illustrative figures. Whatever the form of the final scheme, it would in part depend on the extent to which the withdrawal of the tax benefit welfare state was matched by the government's desire to reduce direct taxation and the extent to which the tax reform contributed towards paying for the reform of the traditional welfare state. Moreover, it is possible to design a scheme by which the vanishing exemption operated much more gently and over much wider bands of income. The effect, however, would be the same. No matter what kind of vanishing exemption scheme was finally adopted, the reversal to the pre-1920 system of income tax in this country would allow those on low income to be totally exempt from tax while preventing any concessions to those on lower incomes accruing to those further up the income scale. Moreover, once an exemption scheme was decided upon, the government would also have the revenue to allow the introduction of many more bands of tax and so introduce a truly progressive form of direct taxation. For example, it would be possible to have income tax starting at 10p in the pound and rising by units of 10p up to whatever the top rate of tax was set by the government.

The move to an exemption system for taxation would result not only in ensuring that the poor were exempt from tax, and that the marginal rates of every taxpayer were significantly reduced, but allow the introduction of a unisex tax system. Under the present system of personal allowances, a married woman who is working has equal tax rights to a single taxpayer, yet both of these two groups are less favourably treated than the married man. Because there will be a considerable increase in revenue from replacing the personal allowance system by an exemption system, the resources will be available for the introduction of a unisex tax system whereby each taxpayer is taxed as

though a single person. In addition, the resources will be
available to meet a second unfairness of the present system.
Two-wage-earning households not only have higher
average incomes than households with a single-wage
earner, but also have a higher amount of their income
exempt from tax. The majority of families who find themselves dependent on a single wage packet are usually those
who are caring for young children or an aged relative. This
unfairness will be met by the proposal made earlier for the
introduction of a home responsibility payment together
with a much more generous system of child benefits.

A policy of cash limits will have an immediate effect on
the tax benefit welfare state. Changes in the rules whereby
company welfare is paid for out of post-tax income will
have a similar effect on the growth of the company welfare
state. The introduction of an exemption system could be
designed in such a way as to bring about a major redistribution of post-tax income. Moreover, there is a case for dis-
allowing the private welfare educational system the rights
and income which accrues to it under charity law. These
changes will begin to curtail expenditure on the private
welfare state. We therefore need to turn our attention
finally to tax reforms in relation to the fifth welfare state.

(v) *Spreading wealth*

The fifth welfare state results from the very unequal
distribution of wealth in our society and from the income
which results from these wealth holdings. As the Meade
Committee observed, 'Capital produces an income which,
unlike earning capacity, does not decline with age and is
not gained at the expense of leisure.'[18] Wealth can be taxed
in three ways: on its increase in value (capital gains tax);
on its capital value – either annually or when it is transferred (death duties – now replaced by capital transfer tax);
or on its income (as unearned income). All three forms of
taxation are employed in Britain, but they have not resulted

in any marked shift in the distribution of wealth from rich to poor people (as opposed to, in Tony Atkinson's words, from the super-rich to the rich). Nor have those assets which give rise to a regular income been redistributed to any marked extent.

The estate duty tax was introduced in 1894 as 'a means of redressing social inequalities'. The tax never lived up to these expectations and, as John Kay and Mervin King have waggishly commented, 'the healthy, wealthy and well advised' have been able to order their tax affairs in such a way as to avoid paying estate duty almost completely.[19] The accuracy of this statement can be seen by looking at the actual revenue raised from capital taxation. In 1968/9, estate duty raised £382 million. By 1978/9 the total had fallen to £369 million. In real terms the fall is much greater, of course; not surprisingly, therefore, while estate duty contributed 5·8 per cent of total revenue in 1968/9, its contribution amounted to only 1·5 per cent a decade later.

It has been argued that one reason why the revenue raised from taxation has declined in real terms is that wealth is now much more evenly spread, but, as we saw in Chapter 1, this is not supported by the evidence. Moreover, as Tony Atkinson has shown, in 1927, when the top nominal rates of estate duty stood at around 30 per cent, death duties represented just 0·42 per cent of all personal wealth holdings.[20] Making a similar calculation for 1976 gives the revenue from estate duty and capital transfer tax together amounting to only 0.2 per cent of total personal wealth.[21]

Since the marginal rates of capital taxation have been increased significantly this century, one would have expected a very much larger revenue to have been gained than appears in the Revenue figures. The size of the discrepancy has been highlighted by Tony Atkinson who has estimated 'that had the 1966 rates of duty been in force in 1911 (with the exemption level and the tax brackets the same percentage of average wealth), the revenue payable would have been 1·5 per cent of total personal wealth. This is nearly four times the actual percentage collected in 1966, and would have implied a revenue in 1966 of some £1200 million rather than the actual revenue of £300 million.'[22] Using the same approach, Pond and his colleagues calculated that in 1977/8 the expected revenue from capital taxation 'would have been over £3000 million. The actual revenue from estate duty in 1974/5 was £398 million – one-eighth as much as these calculations would predict.'[23] The establishment of discretionary trusts and the use of lifetime gifts have played a key part in protecting the concentration of wealth in few hands.

While estate duty was replaced by the capital transfer tax in 1975 it is unlikely to be more effective in re-distributing wealth. Originally, an exemption level was set at £15,000, but shortly afterwards it was raised to £25,000. In addition, so many concessions have been made to the scheme's effectiveness that 'over a ten-year period a couple could pass on more than £100,000 without paying a penny in tax.' And this calculation takes account neither of the gifts allowed in consideration of marriage[24] nor of the fact that since the 1980 Budget the exemption limit has been doubled to £50,000.

The Finance Act of 1965 introduced a capital gains tax in order to tax the appreciation of wealth at a time when an asset changes hands. Important exceptions were made to the comprehensiveness of the tax by exempting a person's only or main residence, a certain range of personal possessions, together with private motor cars. That this tax, too, has been successfully negotiated by tax lawyers can be seen from the contribution it makes to the Exchequer. In 1974/5 the capital gains tax contributed £382 millions to the Exchequer. By 1978/9 this had fallen to £353. In the former year, capital gains contributed 2·7 per cent of revenue raised, but only 1·6 per cent by 1978/9.

Up until 1973 the principle that earned income should be taxed more lightly than unearned income was achieved by providing an earned income relief together with a special surcharge on investment income. Unearned income is at present taxed at an additional 15 per cent on top of the relevant marginal tax rate which the taxpayer would face on earned income. But the surcharge of 15 per cent applies only to investment income in excess of £5000. Moreover, this rate applies to £5000 of taxable unearned income and so all the tax deductions for which a taxpayer might be eligible are taken into account before computing the tax rate.

(a) Wealth tax

A reform of capital taxation is therefore urgent and should be formulated along lines which take into account the principles outlined in the Introduction. A traditionally envisaged wealth tax would reduce wealth inequalities but at the cost of transferring individual wealth to the state. So as to spread wealth more evenly throughout the community, Cedric Sandford and his colleagues suggest the introduction of an accessions tax. Such a tax, while partly operating by the transfer of assets from the private to the public sector, also reduces inequality by offering wealth holders an incentive to spread their wealth within the private sector.[25] And while an accessions tax can be weighted so that the tax on wealth is levied inversely to the wealth holdings of the recipient, such an innovation could be rigged to favour spreading wealth within families – by transference to grandchildren or, in some cases, great-grandchildren – rather than between rich and not-so-rich householders. On balance, therefore, there is a case for considering an annual wealth tax, the funds of which are used to pay out universal capital grants to the population at different stages of the life cycle. The two most obvious stages at which people could most benefit from an injection of capital are when they marry, and when they retire. Indeed, as wealth becomes more evenly spread there will be less need for a capital gift at the period of retirement.

Ironically, most people seem to believe that the distribution of wealth is fair, justifying it with such phrases as 'Well, he has earned it.' We have already seen that this is far from the truth. But the gut reaction that people have 'earned it', together with the view that unless other measures were also taken, the revenue from a wealth tax would be 'lost' in the Exchequer, accounts for the low political appeal of capital tax changes. A reform which was linked to the payment of capital grants could prove to be an effective way of galvanizing widespread support for a wealth tax. Even so, the tax needs to be seen as one part of a comprehensive programme of fiscal reform – a lesson learned from Labour's last incursion into this field.[26]

(b) *New capital gains tax*

In addition, the rules for exemption for capital gains tax should be tightened. In particular, the tax should apply to part of the capital gains from owner-occupation. We have seen that the owner-occupier gains three tax subsidies: tax relief on mortgage interest relief, the abolition of the Schedule A tax on imputed rent, while also being exempt from capital gains tax. There are powerful political and logical reasons why a policy of cash ceilings on mortgage interest relief should not be accompanied by a re-introduction of Schedule A tax. However, the same arguments do not apply to extending the capital gains tax, at least in part, to owner-occupation. For most people, the ownership of a house is their major capital asset. Given that this book has argued for a wider distribution of wealth which gives individuals power over their own lives and a stake in the community, I believe it would be wrong to apply the revamped tax to the whole of the capital gains accruing from owner-occupation. Rather, some of the capital gains should be kept by individuals. The suggestion is that a capital gain of £10,000, or a doubling of the original price paid for the house, whichever is the greater, should be the exemption limits for the capital gains tax. The effect of these proposals would be to exempt many owner-occupiers while taxing the excessive capital gains enjoyed by those who are often at the top end of the income scale.

Conclusion

This chapter has outlined a reform of Britain's five welfare states. A total reform is required not only on grounds of equity but in order to release the financial resources for overhauling the traditional benefit welfare state. Here the key reform – the payment of a generous child benefit – is one which aims at transforming the position of children in our society. Without this change, many of the other benefit reforms will be seen as unfair by much of the electorate. In addition, it is proposed to keep the national insurance system of benefits but with three fundamental changes. First, it is proposed that the contributions for benefit be converted into a progressive social security tax. Secondly, the contributory requirements for benefits will be kept to the very minimum. Thirdly, benefits will be paid for as long as need lasts, and at the higher rate of national insurance benefits for long-term claimants. These reforms will in particular help the unemployed and the long-term sick. In addition, it is proposed to introduce a new benefit for single-parent families.

The reversal of the Thatcher government's tax concessions to the rich will free the resources to begin implementing this programme, particularly the increases in child benefit. But further resources will be required – hence the relevance of reforming the other four welfare states. An immediate move is to limit the value of all tax benefits to the standard rate of tax. It is then proposed that many of the tax benefits should have a policy of cash ceilings applied against them. Similarly, benefits provided by companies will have to be paid for out of post-tax income. The reform of capital taxation will play a major part in equalizing the distribution of wealth. But the most fundamental reform proposed in the book is the re-introduction of an exemption system for taxation – on a modified basis. Such a reform will massively increase the amount of income subject to tax. This will allow the overhauling of the traditional benefit welfare state, while at the same time cutting the rates of taxation for most taxpayers. How feasible a programme this is for the Left in Britain is examined in the final chapter.

12. Home-made Socialism

Is the programme outlined in the last chapter one which the country can afford and which a Labour government might implement? Where the resources could come from to implement these reforms is considered in the first part of this final chapter. It looks at the calculations that Beveridge undertook for implementing his own proposals, as well as the extent to which a reform of the other four welfare states will allow the building-up of the traditional welfare state and simultaneously allow cuts in the rates of income tax. The second part of the chapter examines how receptive the Labour Party might be to these reforms. Conventional wisdom insists that Labour played a key part in bringing about today's traditional benefit welfare state. Does the evidence bear this out? A distinction can be drawn between a certain lack of interest shown by Labour's parliamentary leadership and the more radical views on welfare advanced by the rank and file. But whatever Labour's view has been in the past, there is one key force which will concentrate the party's mind on broadening its appeal. Over the past thirty years Labour has suffered a massive haemorrhage in votes, and if the party is to regain power it will have to rebuild a new coalition of voters. An obvious item in a programme for such a coalition will be the implementation of imaginative welfare reforms to bring about a redistribution of cash resources favouring those on average and below-average incomes; this, then, is the concern of the third and final part of the chapter.

Can we afford it?

This was a question to which Beveridge addressed himself at the height of the Second World War. When reviewing the poverty studies carried out in British towns during the inter-war years, Beveridge was at pains to stress that while in every town surveyed substantial numbers of families had less than the minimum for subsistence, the great bulk of working-class families had 'substantially more than the minimum'.[1] For example, the 1936 poverty study of York showed that those working-class households living above the minimum levels had a total surplus of at least eight times the deficiency of those households in poverty. On the basis of this review, Beveridge went on to conclude:

Want could have been abolished before the present war by redistribution of income within the wage-earning classes, without touching any of the wealthier classes. This is said not to suggest that redistribution of income should be confined to the wage-earning classes; still less is it said to suggest that men should be content with avoidance of poverty, with subsistence income. It is said simply as the most convincing demonstration that abolition of want just before the war was easily within the economic resources of the community; want was a needless scandal due to not taking the trouble to prevent it.[2]

On the effect of rising prosperity, Beveridge was equally clear. Commenting on the rise in real wages during the previous thirty to forty years, he observed that although this had 'diminished want, [it] did not reduce want to insignificance. The moral is that new measures to spread prosperity are needed.'[3] In other words, Beveridge understood only too well that the produce of an ever-rising national income is not automatically spread in such a way as to abolish poverty and the worst forms of inequality. As it is likely that we are now in a world of slow, or possibly nil, economic growth, taking a view of the distribution of existing resources becomes critically important.

National income having more than doubled since the end of the war, it is difficult to argue that the resources are not available to implement an effective benefit welfare state. The case for releasing these resources rests on the arguments about a vertical redistribution of income and a horizontal redistribution of income, together with a policy which limits the growth of the other four welfare states.

There is a moral case for a significant vertical re-distribution of income from rich to poor. The evidence in Chapter 1 of this book shows the marked differences in income and wealth which characterize the post-war period. While the official data end before the advent of the Thatcher government in 1979, one of the first and most significant moves made by the new government was to bring about a major redistribution of income from poorer to richer sections of the community. As we saw in Chapter 6 the tax burden over the past couple of decades increased fastest for the poor and for those with children. Yet these were the two groups who got least from Thatcher's tax cuts. The 1979 Budget brought about a major vertical redistribution of income from poor to rich. The richest 1 per cent of taxpayers cornered 15 per cent of all tax cuts, and the richest 7 per cent picked up 34 per cent of the £4·5 billion cut in direct taxation – a total of £1560 million. The second Thatcher Budget continued this redistribution from those on lower incomes to those at the top of the income scale. Although the tax cuts were more modest than in the 1979 Budget, it was the rich who benefited the most. If the next Labour government were concerned only with redistributing back to the poor the tax concessions made to the very rich, revenue to the Exchequer would be increased by £2 billion at a stroke.

Galvanizing support for a horizontal redistribution of income will require a massive educational programme to encourage people to take a lifetime's view of their income. It is important for everyone to appreciate that their two peak periods in relative affluence are before starting a family (when many people are still living in their parents' home) and when one's own family is grown up and, often, still at home. The periods of relative deprivation are the same today as they were when first highlighted by Rowntree over eighty years ago. The vast majority of families suffer a relative decline in their living standards when they are responsible for children, and again as they move into old age. Part of the financing of the new welfare state will come from spreading a person's income more evenly over their lifetime.

There is also the case for implementing the tax reforms outlined in the previous chapter which would themselves significantly increase the amount of revenue accruing to the Exchequer. Reform of the traditional benefit welfare state – which should be implemented in stages as the money becomes available – could thereby be accompanied by cuts in taxation for those on average and below-average earnings. Resources will be released for the Exchequer by implementing a policy of cash limits in the tax benefit welfare state and allowing company welfare provision to be paid for only out of post-tax income. Massive additional revenue will be forthcoming in a switch from an allowance to an exemption system of personal taxation. In addition, the reform of capital taxation will give rise to additional resources which a future Labour government should redistribute in cash. Part of the cash redistribution would be in the form of adequate welfare benefits, part in using the revenue from the reform of capital taxation to pay capital grants to individuals, and part in accompanying reforms of the other four welfare states with reductions in direct taxation.

Labour's track record

The second question which needs to be considered is, 'Is this a total programme upon which a Labour government will embark?' Richard Crossman once observed that each of the major political parties has a vested interest in promoting various myths about its own record. These myths are important not so much in a party's performance in government, but in mobilizing its supporters during the run-up to a general election. One of Labour's 'myths', and one which is widely believed among Conservatives, is that the party is not only committed to extending the provisions of welfare, but also played a key part in establishing the traditional benefit welfare state. How does this myth stand up to close scrutiny?

While the Labour Party can claim the introduction of much of the traditional welfare state, it neither invented it nor fully understood its importance. One of the best arguments in defence of Labour's social policy record comes from Professor Marwick. In a now much neglected article, Marwick helped shape conventional wisdom by arguing that the Labour Party made a major, and in some ways a unique, contribution to the development of the policies which gave birth to the modern welfare state. In doing so, he showed that Labour set out a comprehensive health service policy thirty years before the introduction of the National Health Service. He goes on to maintain that while Labour's educational demands were somewhat less radical than those on the health service, the party nevertheless made a considerable contribution to the development of today's educational service.[4]

The rest of Labour's record does not, however, support the Marwick thesis about the importance of Labour's contribution towards establishing the welfare state, particularly when the question of income maintenance is considered. Indeed, Marwick argues elsewhere that much of the Coalition and post-war Labour governments' home programme was the product of the new middle-ground social pressure groups of the 1930s.[5] This is a theme which has been taken up and skilfully developed with considerable political insight by Paul Addison.[6]

However, the failure of the Coalition and the Labour governments to advance as fast and as far as circumstances would seem to have allowed can be explained partly by the natural preoccupation of a government at war and by the chaotic conditions of the post-war world. Indeed, these were the overriding problems illustrated in contemporary political biography. Yet a study of Labour's contribution to the ideas which underlined the Beveridge Report shows how right Addison is in maintaining that Labour was the inheritor rather than the initiator of the new post-war consensus. More importantly, it shows how rank-and-file opinion, particularly represented by the Labour Party Conference, was in advance of the parliamentary leadership at that time.

Prior to the 1942 Annual Party Conference (and therefore before the publication of the Beveridge Report itself), Labour published a pamphlet entitled *The Old World and the New Society* which set out the conditions to achieve for Britain, President Roosevelt's four freedoms. These four freedoms, worthy in aspiration but vague in details, were the gaining of full employment, the rebuilding of a better Britain, the provision of social services to secure adequate health, nutrition and care in old age for all, and educational opportunities for everybody. This policy document made no specific mention of the abolition of poverty or of this being one of the party's major goals, let alone how such a goal was to be achieved. One might, of course, argue that this is being too critical of *The Old World and the New Society*, for few Labour Party policy documents make the abolition of poverty a goal – but this is itself significant. Similarly, the document was silent on how welfare reforms were to be paid for and on how the financing of a welfare programme could itself be a major agent for redistribution.

The Old World and the New Society was debated at the 1942 Annual Conference, delegates calling for a specific four-point programme to help secure that new society. The measures demanded were a comprehensive scheme of social security, a scheme of adequate benefits, the introduction of family allowances and the creation of a national health service. Chapter 4 detailed how the Beveridge scheme was faulted at birth by the exclusion of certain groups and the fixing of benefits at too low a level. In re-reading the 1942 Annual Conference debate it is clear that the leadership had no appreciation of how crucial were the terms 'adequate' or 'comprehensive' to the success of the proposed welfare reforms. Indeed, Jim Griffiths, who led for the National Executive Committee (NEC) during the debate, spent most of his time defending family allowances and dwelling on the defects of the current system. More importantly, the NEC did not respond to the questioning by rank and file of the contributory principle and the need for the scheme to be financed totally from the Exchequer.

A similar failure to grasp the essentials of the Beveridge package was demonstrated by Arthur Greenwood when opening the Commons debate on the Report. This debate shows that no government spokesman had any idea of how fundamental were the mere 'details', as they were then being described, of the Beveridge Report. Greenwood spent most of his time confusing what he called the principles of the social security scheme – the introduction of family allowances, the maintenance of full employment and the introduction of a comprehensive health service – with the scheme's details – adequate and comprehensive benefits to be paid to all groups in poverty. Indeed, what was most novel about Greenwood's contribution was his observation that 'the abolition of mass unemployment . . . implies a developing prosperity out of which the funds necessary for the services vital to national well-being can be provided.'[7] In this unnoticed remark, Greenwood laid the basis for a post-war consensus about welfare being paid for out of growth rather than through redistribution.

In marked contrast to the ambiguity of the parliamentary leadership's response was that at the 1944 Labour Party Conference. In a report submitted to the conference, the party set out its reaction to the Beveridge Report and the government's intended plan of action. The report made three points of great importance. On the issue of subsistence benefits, the Labour Party pledged itself 'to work towards the realization of a national minimum standard below which no citizen is allowed to fall.' The document went on to say that the absence of a subsistence basis in the White Paper 'places a heavy responsibility on the government for ensuring a reasonable stability of the price level.'[8]

The document also insisted that benefits should be paid for as long as need lasted. It attacked the limitation of paying unemployment benefit for a thirty-week duration only, and insisted that the commitment to full employment should be accompanied by the abolition of any limitation on unemployment benefit (which is made that much easier in conditions of full employment) as well as the more generous provision of benefits for those who are unemployed. The report also attacked the limitation placed on sickness benefit, linking this argument to the beneficial effects of introducing the National Health Service. Similarly, the report is clear about the provision of benefits for pensioners. It welcomed the agreement to pay pensions at a rate higher than suggested by Beveridge, but decried the government's decision to pay at less than the unemployment and sickness rates.

Why were these views of the rank and file not acted upon? Part of the answer lies in the ease with which the Labour leadership has been able to disregard the discussions of the rank and file. But another, equally important force has been at work. Despite the evidence on the relevance of income maintenance reforms to Labour voters, welfare has never rated as a major political issue to the parliamentary leadership. The almost-zero rating allotted to the major welfare state reforms of the Coalition government and the Attlee administration can be seen from their failure to gain even a reference in the memoirs of the leading Labour politicians of the time. Moreover, this low political importance attached to welfare is reflected in the work of those academic commentators who have written some of the standard biographies of this period.

In the massive biography of Herbert Morrison by Bernard Donaghue and G. W. Jones, only one out of 655 pages of text is devoted to the Beveridge Report. Although the authors mention Morrison's Swindon speech in December 1942 when he called on the nation to look beyond social security, which he described as 'at best nothing more than ambulance and salvage work: rescuing and patching up our social casualties', these ideas are in no way developed. Indeed, a later section of the book shows Morrison's key role in mobilizing support for containing rather than developing Labour policy in the latter stages of the 1945/50 parliament.[9]

While the Morrison biography at least makes a mention of the Beveridge Report, there is not a single entry on this topic in the Dalton memoirs. Similarly, in Colin Cooke's biography of Cripps, Beveridge is mentioned only twice, and then in passing, in references to the effect of the all-party agreement on the range of post-war reforms which were necessary.[10]

Attlee is typically uninterested in the whole issue. Indeed, in his edited Granada Historical Records interview, the then leader of the Labour Party becomes so vague that he fails to mention the Beveridge reforms at all.[11] It could be that Attlee was not asked about Beveridge, but this itself says something about the importance which the interviewer thought the Labour Party attached to these reforms at the time of Attlee's leadership. But this doesn't excuse Attlee for failing to introduce this subject into the conversation if he thought it was important enough.

On another occasion, when specifically prompted by an

interviewer, Attlee was incredibly vague on the ideas and scope of the income maintenance side of the welfare state. At one point in the interview, Attlee recalled that 'Arthur Greenwood [in charge of post-war reconstruction] conceived the idea of a committee to consider necessary changes in national insurance and so on.'[12] Attlee then misleadingly comments: 'But the Beveridge Report was endorsed by the whole Cabinet in its broad lines – there may have been one or two minor points of disagreement.'[13] In his own autobiography, Attlee makes no mention of the report, its contents, or its importance to the building of a new society, except to say that he hoped the plan would be implemented by the Coalition government.[14]

Fortunately this lack of concern was not shared by the entire Parliamentary Labour Party. In his autobiography, Emanuel Shinwell contradicts Attlee's view that Labour was basically agreed on the Coalition government's approach to the Beveridge Report. Shinwell writes, 'the arguments were long and at times somewhat bitter; they continued until the government was forced to say that the report would be implemented at least in part.' The attempt to get the Coalition government to spell out its reaction to the Beveridge scheme during the first parliamentary debate on the Report led to 'the most serious row behind the scenes in which I was involved'.[15] Dalton, in his diaries, observes Shinwell's attempt to organize backbenchers to force a vote in favour of implementing the Beveridge Report in the following terms: 'Master Shinwell today has been rushing about with a maniacal glint in his eye. He reminds me of the chap who was determined to set fire to the house and burn it down for his own delight.'[16] The Coalition government suffered its worst adverse vote following this debate.

The low priority given to welfare reform by the Labour leaderships can be seen from the record of the 1964/70 Labour government. Harold Wilson's own account of this period runs to about 35,000 lines of which less than two dozen are devoted to the national superannuation proposals which were Labour's main social security reform of the period. Indeed, this reform gets the same billing in the Wilson memoirs as does the Salvation Army. The ex-Premier's only comments are to the effect that the super-annuation proposals failed to become law, and with almost half a million words to spare Wilson does not find the space to say that it was his timing of the election which lost the whole of the proposals. (The Bill had not completed its parliamentary passage before the election was called.) Nor is there any mention as to why such a major measure was not taken at the beginning of the parliament.[17]

The Labour governments headed by Harold Wilson and James Callaghan during the 1974/9 period were concerned with the introduction of only three major social security measures. The first was a new pensions plan, which had virtually all-party support; the second was that of linking increases in benefits to prices or earnings – whichever was the most favourable to claimants; and the third concerned the phasing out of child tax allowances and family allow-ances and replacing them with a cash benefit for mothers called child benefits – again, a reform which had all-party support.

The pensions reforms were supported by a powerful trade union, but the low esteem in which most welfare reform is held by leading Labour politicians can be seen from the way the leading members of the Labour Cabinet tried to veto the introduction of the child benefit scheme. On the basis of an alleged survey of backbench MPs' views (which turned out to be the view of the Whips' office and nothing more), leading politicians told their counterparts in the trade union movement that backbenchers were disturbed about the introduction of the child benefit scheme and its repercussions on take-home pay with the loss of child tax allowances. Trade union leaders therefore agreed to a postponement of the scheme. The Labour Cabinet was then told that both trade union leaders and rank-and-file MPs were anxious to see the scheme shelved. It was only when the key papers for this period were leaked and the balloon went up that demands were made for the full implementation of the scheme.[18]

The party's over?

With this past record, what hope is there of getting the Labour Party to implement the proposals suggested in this book? A note of optimism can be struck from the evidence so far presented. In each of the crucial stages over the past forty years or so, Labour Party rank-and-file members have attempted to tie the parliamentary leadership to a programme which held out the possibility of a successful attack on poverty and inequality. The current moves to increase the influence of the rank and file could therefore work in favour of a radical commitment to reforming welfare in this country.

Moreover, the Labour leaderships' failure to see the importance to Labour voters of welfare reforms was largely the result of the priorities of a party born from the trade union movement with its interests naturally concentrated on the industrial front. Yet even here it is important to notice the beginnings of change in the priorities of the trade unions themselves. The 1974 Labour government's social priorities were in large part determined by trade union pressure and the emphasis given to the £10, £16 pension pledge owes almost everything to the efforts of the industrial wing of the Labour movement. In time this change in trade union emphasis will begin to make itself felt in the parliamentary leadership's views and order of priority on other welfare issues.

There is also a further and perhaps even more powerful force working in favour of this programme. If Labour is to win another general election it will need to rebuild and strengthen its support among the electorate. This will only be done by winning new groups of voters which have hitherto given their support to other parties or to none. Such a task is urgent for there is not one but a number of electoral crises besieging the Labour Party. There has been a steady erosion of the party's traditional power-base among certain sections of the electorate. This fall in the numbers of votes cast is beginning to see its effect in the decline of Labour representation in parliament. And as if this were not bad enough, the Labour Party has ceased to be a mass party in the country.

There has been an almost steady decline in Labour's electoral support over the past thirty years. In the 1979 general election the party managed to poll only 28·1 per cent of those eligible to vote. This total is smaller than at any time since the Second World War. Even if we look at Labour's share of those who voted (as opposed to the total electorate) the performance is not much better. In the 1979 election, Labour candidates managed to muster between them only 36·9 per cent of the total votes cast. This is lower than at any post-war election and is worse than the party's performance in the general election of 1935.

The electoral crisis facing the Labour Party is more visible if we look at the number of people voting Labour in post-war elections. Labour polled almost 12 million votes in 1945. This rose by over a million in the 1950 election, rising again to almost 14 million in 1951. This marks the high point in Labour's electoral appeal. Apart from 1966, Labour's vote has steadily fallen. This is serious enough, but it becomes doubly so when we look at the size of the electorate over the same period of time. Labour's vote in the 1979 election was less than the number of votes cast for Labour candidates in 1945, but in the intervening years the electorate had grown by well over 6 million voters.

There are three main waves of support among the electorate for Labour candidates. Labour polls well in the big cities. Indeed, Labour's safe seats are heavily concentrated in the inner city. In the last election Labour candidates were three times more likely to score success in a large city seat than their Conservative opponents, and well over a third of Labour's representation in parliament comes from such seats. But many of these constituencies have small electorates and will disappear under the Boundary Commission proposals which are likely to be implemented before the next election. On a conservative estimate, Labour is likely to lose twenty seats from redistribution alone.

A second source of Labour support comes from trade unionists. The Parliamentary Labour Party was largely created by the trade unions, and not unnaturally Labour candidates draw heavily for their support from trade unionists and their families. Yet 1979 was the first year in which Labour's share of the trade union vote fell to 50 per cent – a fall of 5 percentage points from the previous election. And while it was an exaggerated claim that half the trade unionists voted Tory in the last election, Margaret Thatcher scored a considerable success in winning 31 per cent of trade unionists' votes – up 8 percentage points on the previous election.

The third source of Labour support comes from what sociologists crudely call the lower social groups – manual workers and the poor. These groups vote handsomely for Labour candidates and, overwhelmingly, Labour support comes from these groups. But two changes threaten Labour's vote here. First, of these groups which poll heavily for Labour, manual workers are a shrinking proportion of the total electorate. So even if the same proportion vote for Labour, there will be fewer votes cast at the end of the day. Second, even among this smaller group of the electorate, Labour's vote began to collapse at the last election. The swing to the Conservatives since 1974 among skilled workers was 10 per cent while a 9-per-cent swing was recorded to the Conservatives among the unskilled and the poor.

The decline in the Labour vote may be temporarily reversed by a backlash against the Thatcher government, but even here the word 'may' must be emphasized. By 1983 the Thatcher administration will have massive receipts from the North Sea oil revenues. The size of the oil tax revenue alone will allow for a major tax cut. On past performance it is clear that the government will cut back public expenditure still further if this is necessary to gain the resources to make further cuts in direct taxation in the run-up to the next election. The Labour Party must therefore command a wider basis of support if it is to secure its future and so prevent a break-up of the political system into a whole range of splinter parties.

Despite the failure of Labour leadership over many generations to realize the importance of income maintenance proposals to many sections of Labour voters, I believe this is one issue on which Labour could begin to rebuild support among the electorate for, above all, these policies are about extending the personal freedom of the majority of voters. The programme is about transferring money from rich to poor and from the state to the individual. The reforms aim to give people the power to direct their own lives rather than being in the receipt of welfare services which are centrally directed. The programme is also a plea about taking an overall view of one's lifetime's income and needs and showing that at crucial times these do not match one another. Above all, these policies also have a crucial role in strengthening the rights of women and children in our society.

Conclusion

This book has been concerned with exploring the basis of and the policies by which a fundamental reform of Britain's five welfare states can be brought about. Today the traditional welfare state not only fails to combat poverty but all too often operates as a ceiling, making it impossible for the poor to escape from their poverty. The transformation of the traditional benefit welfare state proposed here will not only eradicate poverty as it is known today, but will simultaneously restructure welfare so as to provide a minimum floor on which people can build by their own efforts. The proposals are aimed at increasing the power of the individual by giving people cash benefits as of right which will allow them a far greater say in running their own lives. This is in contrast to the discriminatory and off-hand treatment meted out to many claimants today and the cynicism with which the poor are often treated.

Moreover, by proposing welfare reforms which build on what is already in existence, and working with the grain of human nature rather than against it, the programme is essentially one of home-made socialism. While the funds for the first part of the reforms will be gained by reversing the Thatcher government's massive tax concessions to the rich, expenditure on Britain's four other welfare states needs to be controlled if the resources are going to be secured for rebuilding anew the traditional benefit welfare state.

There are important political grounds for believing that this programme can be implemented by a future Labour government. Many of the 28 per cent of the electorate who voted Labour last time are poor, and this programme has an immediate attraction to them. But a policy of home-made socialism could have an appeal to people much further up the income scale. The policies themselves must be seen as part of a wide and necessary attack by Labour on the centralization of power. Welfare reform has a crucial role in transferring cash from the state to the individual, from rich to poor, from men to women as well as from adults to children. Home-made socialism is essentially about extending freedom, not of the few but of the many.

Appendix I: Costs

This appendix estimates, as far as it is possible to do so, the costs of the social security reforms outlined in Chapter 11. I am grateful to the DHSS for supplying this information. The Department has been unable to give the costs of each reform on the same price basis.

REFORM 1

The cost of raising child benefits to the child addition rate paid to the children of claimants on the short-term national insurance benefits at November 1980 benefit rates is £690 million net (after taking into account saving on other children's benefits).

REFORM 2

The only reform which is advocated in advance of paying a much higher child benefit concerns the payment of unemployment benefit. To pay the flat rate benefit for as long as unemployment lasts is in the order of £100 million at average benefit rates for the 1980/1 financial year.

REFORM 3

The cost of increasing child benefit to the additional rate paid to the children of higher rate national insurance beneficiaries to make the benefit taxable is £4315 million net.

REFORM 4

The fourth reform is to pay the higher rate of national insurance benefit to those unemployed who have been without work for over a year. The cost of this reform is in the order of £175 million if the level of benefit corresponds to the rate of invalidity pension and assuming the average benefit levels for 1980/1.

REFORM 5

The DHSS has been unable to estimate the net cost of paying a single parent family allowance at the non-contributory invalidity benefit level. The gross cost is put at £375 million in November 1978 figures. The net cost will be significantly below this level, for the DHSS has calculated the net cost of paying the single parent allowance at this level together with the higher national insurance rates for children at £250 million.

REFORM 6

This reform is to pay the single-parent-family allowance at the higher rate of national insurance benefits and the net cost is estimated at £160 million in November 1978 benefit figures.

REFORM 7

The next two reforms cover disabled people. The cost of extending the non-contributory invalidity pension (the non-contributory as well as the housewife's non-contributory invalidity pension (NCIP and HNCIP)) by scrapping the household duties test is £250 million at the benefit rates introduced in November 1979.

REFORM 8

The cost of paying the NCIP and HNCIP beneficiaries at the rate for invalidity pension is about £130 million, again at November 1979 benefit rates. Extending this coverage to those who would qualify if the household duties test were abolished would cost £290 million. In addition, the cost of paying invalidity allowance, where appropriate, to those beneficiaries would be about an extra £150 million.

REFORM 9

It was suggested in the text that a £600 million input be given to a pensioner tax credit.

Some of the cost of implementing these proposals will come from reversing the major redistribution to the rich brought about in the first two years of the Thatcher government. Since the 1979 and 1980 tax cuts favoured the childless taxpayer there is a powerful case for channelling any net revenue derived from overturning these budgets into the pockets of families with children. The case for such action becomes overwhelming when one considers the discrimination against families which has built up in this fiscal system since the mid-1950s. Another, not insignificant contribution, will come in savings on staff costs. Means-tested supplementary benefit is immensely expensive to administer. As the programme above is implemented, fewer people will be dependent on supplementary benefits, FIS, rent and rate rebates and so on, with consequential savings on staff time. But the major part of the reforms can only be introduced as the funds become available from the tax changes proposed in the second half of Chapter 11. However, as the tax system is reformed along the lines suggested – and the income of the poor is thereby exempted from tax – all benefits should become part of taxable income. This will ensure that help is concentrated on those in greatest need while at the same time limiting the cost of the reforms.

There may be some criticism about the suggestion that, apart from a small reform on unemployment benefit, Reforms 4 to 8 should await the implementation of a fundamental shift in resources to families by way of child benefits. The temptation to introduce the other reforms first are considerable, particularly as their cost is so much less than the child benefit proposals. But it has been, and will remain a major act of political folly to reform the traditional welfare state without first equalizing the benefit payments to children, irrespective of the status of the parents. Tactically it would be a good move to accompany any major changes in child benefit with the introduction of a pensioner tax credit – but this reform will be dependent more on the Inland Revenue computerization programme than on decisions about need and political presentation.

Appendix II: Back to Beveridge

A number of proposals suggesting radical reforms of the traditional benefit welfare state have been put forward over the past fifteen years and many of these have come from Lord Harris, Arthur Seldon and associates at the Institute of Economic Affairs.[1] There have also been five reports suggesting a 'back to Beveridge' approach, all differing from the one outlined in this book. *Inequality in Britain* attempts to answer the question where the resources can come from to reform welfare, in an age of slow or nil growth, and in a society where there is considerable resistance to increasing the level of direct taxation – at least for those on the standard rate.

The first serious suggestion of returning to Beveridge is to be found in the work of Professor A. B. Atkinson. Way back in 1969 Tony Atkinson concluded a study on the extent of poverty in Britain by proposing the raising of the retirement pension to the subsistence level recommended by Beveridge – or, as we would now say, the supplementary benefit level – together with an increase in family allowances (now called child benefits) to the level of the supplementary rates for children. 'If we were also to increase the other flat-rate national insurance benefits, then these measures taken together can be said to represent a "back to Beveridge" policy for dealing with poverty.'[2]

In 1975 the Child Poverty Action Group (CPAG) returned to this theme by advocating a more comprehensive revamping of the Beveridge scheme. The aim of these proposals was 'to ensure an adequate income *as of right* to those groups unable to earn such an income. This, we believe, can best be achieved through the reform and extension of the existing national insurance scheme.' In support of these proposals the Group quoted the key passage with which Beveridge had begun his own report;

> to prevent interruption or destruction of earning power from leading to want, it is necessary to improve the present scheme of social insurance in three directions: by extension of scope to cover persons now excluded, by extension of purpose to cover risks now excluded, and by raising the rates of benefits.[3]

1978 saw the publication of two reports advocating a back to Beveridge approach. As part of the major review of taxation and benefits in this country, the Meade Committee on the Structure and Reform of Direct Taxation surveyed the current proposals for reforming the social security system. Two proposals were examined in detail: a two-tier social dividend scheme and a new Beveridge Scheme. After examining these two options the report opted for a new Beveridge scheme, adding:

> This implies: (i) raising tax thresholds to avoid the increasing threat of overlap between the levels of supplementary benefit and the levels of income at which tax may start to be charged; (ii) setting the regular National Insurance and similar benefits at levels comparable to supplementary benefit levels; (iii) relying on child benefits for the support of children; (iv) submitting social benefits other than child benefits to tax; and (v) thus enabling a host of present means-tested benefits to be discontinued.

The report went on to advocate a number of tax proposals including the abolition of the present allowances for married couples 'so that at the most two single person's allowances could be claimed against the couple's total income. A more radical reform will be to abolish the married man's allowance in all cases and also to permit the personal tax allowances to be set only against earned income and not against investment income.'[4]

Also, in 1978, the Outer Circle Policy Unit published a report entitled *Beyond Beveridge*. The report, which was the product of a working party set up by the Unit, began by looking at the need for reform and went on to discuss four major reforms of the social security system. The group producing the report listed twelve objectives which any anti-poverty strategy should attempt to achieve. These included the abolition of means tests, raising claimants off supplementary benefits, not imposing high marginal tax rates, concentrating resources on those on low incomes, making allowances for different family responsibilities as well as designing a scheme which was moderately simple.

The working party then looked at the various proposals for reform to see which fulfilled these objectives. In its report the working party came down in favour of a Beveridge-type reform and explained its reasons in the following terms: 'while there is no perfect policy, that is, one free from cost, we would submit that a universalist Beyond Beveridge strategy contains fewer insurmountable costs than either of the alternatives.'[5]

The most recent back-to-Beveridge report comes from the pen of Hermione Parker. Her report published in 1980 by the Outer Circle Policy Unit looks at those measures taken by the Thatcher government which begin dismantling the traditional benefit welfare state – hence its title *Goodbye Beveridge?* This analysis leads Hermione Parker to conclude that

What is really needed, rather than the present ad hoc changes, is a *full-scale Beveridge-style enquiry*, going back to first principles, redefining the objectives of income maintenance and income redistribution programmes, finding out why so many people have to come to depend on supplementary benefit when that was never the intention, and putting forward proposals for radical reform of the whole edifice of taxation, welfare and wages.[6]

The plea for a new Beveridge scheme does not prevent Mrs Parker from then going on to make suggestions about the need for increased family support, decreasing the numbers on means-tested assistance, the training and education allowances for young people, as well as laying down some principles for tax reform and the need for family budgets.

Notes

Introduction

1. Barnes, S., 'Life with a Cabinet Minister: 2', *Sunday Times*, 15 October 1978.
2. Marquand, D., Eighth Rita Hinden Memorial Lecture, 'Taming Leviathan: Social Democracy and Decentralisation', *Socialist Commentary*, 1980, p. 8.
3. Blake, Lord and Patten, J., *The Conservative Opportunity*, Macmillan, 1976.
4. Titmuss, R. M., 'The Social Division of Welfare' in *Essays on the 'Welfare State'*, Allen & Unwin, 1958, which discusses three welfare states.

1. Poverty and Riches

1. Streatfeild, N., *The Day Before Yesterday*, Collins, 1956, pp. 11–12.
2. *The Perception of Poverty in Europe*, Commission of the European Communities, 1977.
3. Tawney, R. H., 'Poverty as an Industrial Problem' in *Memorandum on the Problems of Poverty*, William Morris Press, 1913
4. Royal Commission, Report No. 1, Cmnd 6171, 1975, p. 43.
5. Taken from *The Wealthy*, CIS, 1980, p. 20.
6. Crine, S., 'Pick-Pocketing the Low Paid', *Low Pay Report*, 1, August 1980.
7. Pond, C., Burghes, L. and Smith B., *Taxing Wealth Inequalities*, Fabian tract 466, 1980, p. 4.
8. Atkinson, A. B., *Unequal Shares*, Allen Lane, 1972, p. 22.

2. What Is Poverty?

1. Townsend, P., *Poverty in the United Kingdom*, Allen Lane, 1979.

2. Quoted in Atkinson, A. B., *The Economics of Inequality*, OUP, 1975, p. 189.

3. Simey, T. S. and M. B., *Charles Booth*, OUP, 1960, p. 184.

4. Booth, C., 'The Inhabitants of the Tower Hamlets School Board Division', *Journal of the Royal Statistical Society*, vol. L, 1887, p. 328.

5. Booth, C., 'Conditions and Occupations of the People of East London and Hackney, 1887', *Journal of the Royal Statistical Society*, vol. LI, 1888, p. 278.

6. This view, which is based on the work of Professor and Mrs Simey, has not gone unchallenged. E. P. Hennock argues that the Booth Survey was not undertaken to challenge the SDF's survey – of which no copy now exists – nor was he surprised by his findings. For full details, see 'Poverty and Social Theory in England: the Experiences of the 1880s', *Social History*, January 1976.

7. See Wilson, J., *CB: A Life of Sir Henry Campbell-Bannerman*, Constable, 1973, p. 391, on how quickly this approach paid dividends.

8. Rowntree, B. Seebohm, *Poverty: A Study of Town Life*, Macmillan, 1902 edition, pp. 86–7.

9. For a fuller debate see Field, F., *Poverty, Politics and Power*, Heinemann, forthcoming.

10. Bowley, A. L., *The Measurement of Social Phenomena*, P. S. King & Sons, 1923, pp. 170–1.

11. Rowntree, B. Seebohm, *The Human Needs of Labour*, Thomas Nelson & Sons, 1918.

12. Rowntree, B. Seebohm, *The Human Needs of Labour*, Longmans, Green & Co., 1937 edition.

13. For criticism of this point see Field, F., op. cit.

14. idem.

15. Hancock, W. K. and Gowing, M. M., *British War Economy*, HMSO, 1975, p. 541.

16. *Social Insurance and Allied Services*, Cmnd 6404, 1942, p. 14.

17. For the inside story on the publicity launch, readers should look at Longford, F. (Packenham), *Born to Believe*, Cape, 1953, Chapter 15.

18. For the details see Field, F., op. cit.

19. SBC, *Low Incomes*, HMSO, 1977, p. 23.

20. Walker, C. and Church, M., 'Poverty by Administration', *Journal of Human Nutrition*, vol. 32, pp. 15–16.

21. SBC, *Handbook*, HMSO, 1977, p. 26.

3. The Poor

1. The argument for taking a more generous definition of poverty than I have used is to be found in Townsend, P., *Poverty in the United Kingdom*, op. cit.
2. See Winyard, S., *No Fault of Their Own*, Liverpool Institute of Socio-Religious Studies, 1977.
3. *DE Gazette*, March 1980, p. 318, figures derived.
4. Reproduced as table 5.19 in *Social Trends 10*, HMSO, 1980.
5. *Monthly Digest of Statistics*, HMSO, February 1980, table 3.14.
6. One-parent Families, *Annual Report 1979*.
7. Leete, Richard, 'One-parent Families: Numbers and Characteristics', *Population Trends 13*, HMSO, Autumn 1978.
8. Nixon, J., *Fatherless Families on FIS*, HMSO, 1979, pp 149–50.
9. *Report of the Committee on One-parent Families*, Cmnd 5629, HMSO, 1974, p. 265.
10. One-parent Families, op. cit.
11. GHS, 1976, table 8.8.
12. See 'The Cost of a Comprehensive Disability Allowance' in *Disability Rights Guide*, Disability Alliance, 1979, p. 40.
13. Harris, A. L. *et al.*, *Handicapped and Impaired in Great Britain*, HMSO, 1971, p. 60.
14. Harris, A. L., *Income and Entitlement to Supplementary Benefit of Impaired People in Great Britain*, HMSO, 1972, p. 17.
15. Disability Alliance, *Poverty and Disability*, 1975.
16. The definition includes the pay both of men and of women.
17. For a summary on how the definition of household, manual earnings and the like affects the size of this group, see Field, F., op. cit.
18. *Loving Trap*, National Council for the Single Woman and Her Dependants, 1979, p. 1.
19. Arnold, R., 'The Inequitable Treatment of Those Caring for the Elderly and Infirm', *Poverty*, 28, 1974.
20. Disability Alliance, *Poor People in Hospital*, 1976.
21. See Royal Commission, Report No. 6, Cmnd 7175, 1978.
22. DHSS press release, 19 April 1970.
23. Cmnd 782.
24. Fiegehen, G. C., Lansley, P. S. and Sm⬛⬛⬛⬛⬛ ⬛⬛erty

and Progress in Great Britain, 1953–1973, CUP, 1977, p. 29.
25. Royal Commission, Report No. 6, op. cit., p. 18.
26. The DHSS has records of transferring 90,000 pensioners to rent and rate rebates.

4. What Went Wrong?

1. *Poverty: Ten Years After Beveridge*, PEP, 1952, p. 23.
2. ibid., p. 25.
3. *Social Insurance and Allied Services*, op. cit., p. 7.
4. ibid., pp. 7–8.
5. Harris, J., *William Beveridge*, OUP, 1977, p. 402.
6. 'Basic Problems of Social Security with Heads of a Scheme', Cabinet Papers 87/76, 11 December 1941.
7. Harris, op. cit., p. 403.
8. *Social Insurance and Allied Services*, p. 108.
9. ibid., p. 109.
10. Harris, op. cit., p. 405.
11. ibid., p. 407.
12. *Social Insurance and Allied Services*, p. 124.
13. Cmnd 7054, p. 29.
14. *Social Insurance and Allied Services*, p. 38.
15. 'Basic Problems of Social Security with Heads of a Scheme', op. cit.
16. ibid., p. 31.
17. Cmnd 6404, p. 78.
18. Rowntree, B. Seebohm, 'Poverty and the Beveridge Plan', *The Fortnightly*, February 1943, p. 77.
19. Rowntree, B. Seebohm, 'The Beveridge Plan', *The Friend*, 11 December 1942, p. 712.
20. *The Fortnightly*, op. cit., p. 78.
21. *The Friend*, op. cit., p. 712.
22. Harris, op. cit., p. 408.
23. Beveridge, W., *Power and Influence*, Hodder & Stoughton, 1953, p. 309.
24. Cabinet Papers, 87/79, 1942.
25. Owen, A. D. K., *A Survey of the Standard of Living in Sheffield*, Social Survey Committee, 1933.
26. J. Inman, *Poverty and Housing Conditions in a Manchester Ward*, Manchester University Press, 1934.
27. *A Social Survey of Plymouth*, P. S. King & Sons, 1935.

28. Tout, H., *The Standard of Living in Bristol*, Arrowsmith, 1938, p. 35.
29. ibid., p. 37.
30. *The Fortnightly*, op. cit., p. 1945.
31. *Social Insurance and Allied Serivices*, p. 89.
32. ibid., p. 156.
33. Packenham, F., *Born to Believe*, op. cit.
34. *Hansard*, 18 February 1943, col. 2038–9.
35. ibid., col. 2042.
36. ibid., cols. 2042–3.
37. ibid., col. 2041.
38. Arthur Marwick's title; see his *Britain in the Century of Total War: War, Peace and Social Change, 1900–1967*, Bodley Head, 1968.
39. ibid., p. 315.
40. Bullock, A., *Bevin*, vol. 2, Heinemann, 1967, p. 325.
41. *Social Insurance*, Cmnd 6550, 1944, p. 7.
42. ibid., p. 21.
43. ibid., p. 129.
44. ibid., p. 57.
45. ibid., p. 17.
46. ibid., p. 29.
47. ibid., p. 10.
48. Hood, K., *Room at the Bottom*, Lawrence & Wishart, 1960, pp. 14–15.

5. Who Pays? – National Insurance Fund

1. *Social Insurance and Allied Services*, op. cit., p. 107.
2. *Social Insurance*, op. cit.
3. How the national insurance system redistributes from the employed to the self-employed contributors, and from single persons to married couples, is examined in Michael Reddins's essay, 'National Insurance and Private Pensions' in Jones, K. *et al.*, *Social Policy Year Book 1976*, Routledge & Kegan Paul, 1977.
4. See Kincaid, J. C., *Poverty and Inequality in Britain*, Penguin, 1973, for a more detailed discussion.
5. Hood, op. cit., p. 33.
6. *TUC Report*, 1953, p. 141.
7. *TUC Report*, 1954, p.

8. Jackson, D., Turner, H. A. and Wilkinson, F., *Do Trade Unions Cause Inflation?*, CUP, 1972, p. 70.

6. Who Pays? – Taxation

1. *Hansard*, 12 June 1979, col. 250.
2. *New Statesman*, 4 May 1979.
3. *Hansard*, 9 May 1980, col. 32.
4. Peacock, A. and Shannon, R., 'The Welfare State and the Redistribution of Incomes', *Westminster Bank Review*, 1968, pp. 30–46.
5. Nicholson, J. L. and Britton, A. J. C., 'The Redistribution of Income' in Atkinson A. B. (ed.), *The Personal Distribution of Incomes*, Allen & Unwin, 1979, p. 325.
6. Peretz, J., 'Beneficiaries of public expenditure: an analysis for 1971/1972', mimeograph, nd.
7. Nissel, M., *Taxes and Benefits: does redistribution help the family?* Policy Studies Institute, 1978, p. 3.
8. ibid., p. 4.

7. The Tax Allowance Welfare State

1. Cmnd 7439, 1979, p. 18.
2. Surrey, S. S., 'Tax Expenditure Analysis, the Concept and its Uses', *Canadian Taxation*, vol. 1, no. 2, 1979, p. 5.
3. Willis, J. R. M. and Hardwick, P. J. W., *Tax Expenditures in the United Kingdom*, Heinemann, 1978, p. 1.
4. ibid., p. 16.
5. *Inland Revenue Statistics 1979*, HMSO, 1979, Table 1.8.
6. Cmnd 7841, table 5.13.
7. *Tax Expenditures in the United Kingdom*, op. cit., p. 47.
8. idem.
9. Cmnd 7841, March 1980, table 5.13.
10. *The Hidden Welfare State*, National Council of Welfare, Canada, 1976, p. 16.
11. ibid., p. 17.

8. The Company Welfare State

1. Royal Commission, Report No. 8, Cmnd 7679, 1979, p. 130.

2. Royal Commission, Report No. 3, Cmnd 6383, p. 93.
3. ibid., p. 94.
4. Government Actuary, *Occupational Pensions*, HMSO, 1975, p. 17.
5. ibid., p. 21.
6. Royal Commission, Report No. 3, op. cit., p. 97.
7. ibid., p. 102.
8. *Occupational Pensions*, op. cit., p. 49.
9. Quoted in *Income During Initial Sickness: A New Strategy*, Cmnd 7864, HMSO, 1980, p. XIII.
10. ibid., p. XIV.
11. ibid., p. XVI.
12. Royal Commission, Report No. 8, op. cit., p. 127.
13. Cmnd 7864, op. cit., p. 1.
14. ibid., p. 22.
15. Royal Commission, Report No. 3, p. 208.
16. *Guardian*, 27 December 1974.
17. IDS Study 214, March 1980, p. 7.
18. Royal Commission, Report No. 3, table HC, p. 212.
19. *Financial Times*, 5 February 1979.
20. IDS, op. cit., p. 12.
21. ibid., p. 17.
22. Royal Commission, Report No. 3, p. 215.
23. Reported in *The Times*, 9 December 1976.
24. Royal Commission, Report No. 3, p. 218.
25. IDS, op. cit., p. 14.
26. Royal Commission, Report No. 3, table 49, p. 97.

9. Inherited Power and Welfare

1. Gore, Charles (ed.), *Property*, Macmillan, 1913, p. 10.
2. 'The Distribution of Personal Wealth in Britain', *Bulletin of the Oxford University Institute of Economics and Statistics*, February 1961.
3. 'Assets and Age', *Bulletin of the Oxford University Institute of Economics and Statistics*, August 1962.
4. Reported in Atkinson, A. B., *Unequal Shares*, op. cit., pp. 30–1.
5. Pond, C., Burghes, L. and Smith, B., *Taxing Wealth Inequalities*, op. cit., p. 7.
6. Atkinson, A. B., *Unequal Shares*, op. cit., p. 37.

7. See, for example, the calculations in Fleming, J. S. and Little, I. M. D., *Why We Need a Wealth Tax*, Methuen, 1974.
8. Royal Commission, Report No. 5, Cmnd 6999, 1977, p. 292.
9. *SSRC Newsletter*, 40, October 1979, p. 15.
10. Harbury, C. and Hitchens, D., 'The Myth of the Self-made Man', *New Statesman*, 15 February 1980.

10. The Private Market Welfare State

1. Lee, M., *Private and National Health Services*, PEP, Planning, vol. XLIV, 1978, p. 7.
2. ibid., p. 8.
3. ibid., p. 9.
4. *Guardian*, 30 January 1980.
5. *Guardian*, 31 July 1979.
6. Report of the Royal Commission on the NHS, Cmnd 7615, 1979, p. 293.
7. ibid., p. 290.
8. Public Schools Commission Report, vol. 11, HMSO, 1968, p. 101.
9. Civil Service Commission, *Report of the Committee on the Selection Procedure for the Recruitment of Administration Trainees*, HMSO, 1979, p. 29.
10. Reported in *The Times*, 18 December 1979.
11. See Rogers, R., 'The Myth of the "Independent" Schools', *New Statesman*, 4 January 1980. This section draws heavily from this work.
12. *TES*, 21 March 1980.
13. *Hansard*, 12 February 1980, col. 1465.
14. Glenister, H. and Wilson, G., *Paying for Private Schools*, Allen Lane, 1970.

11. Freedom First: a Programme of Reform

1. See Burghes, Louie, '*So Who's Better Off on the Dole?*', CPAG, 1980, and Supplementary Benefits Commission *Annual Report 1979*, Cmnd 8033, 1980, pp. 39–41.
2. Just how inadequate existing provisions are can be seen in Bruner, J., *Under Five in Britain*, Grant McIntyre, 1980.

3. At this point, and maybe before, there could be a case for taxing child benefit.

4. Rowntree, B. Seebohm, 'Poverty and the Beveridge Plan', *The Fortnightly*, February 1943, p. 80.

5. Foot, M., *Aneurin Bevan*, vol. 1, MacGibbon & Kee, 1962, p. 408.

6. Quoted in Harris, op. cit., p. 423.

7. *National Superannuation*, Labour Party, 1957, p. 10.

8. Hood, op. cit., p. 42.

9. Marwick, A., 'The Labour Party and the Welfare State in Britain 1900–1948', *American Historical Review*, December 1967, p. 401.

10. *Hansard*, 27 June 1980, col. 357–8.

11. ibid., col. 357.

12. These supplements are also paid in addition for the first six months of drawing sickness benefit, industrial injury benefit and widows benefit for those claimants with satisfactory contribution records.

13. 'Cutting Poverty in Half', *One-Parent Times*, no. 1, 1979, p. 13.

14. See in particular *Poverty and Disability: the case for a Comprehensive Income Scheme for Disabled People*, Disability Alliance, 1975.

15. See, for example, Supplementary Benefits Commission, *Annual Report 1977*, Cmnd 7392, HMSO, 1978, p. 58.

16. Field, F. and Townsend, P., *A Social Contract for Families*, CPAG, 1975.

17. Field, F., Meacher, M., Pond, C., *To Him Who Hath: a study of poverty and taxation*, Penguin Books, 1977.

18. Quoted in Pond *et al.*, *Taxing Wealth Inequalities*, op. cit., p. 13.

19. Kay, J. and King, M., *The British Tax System*, OUP, 1978, p. 158.

20. Atkinson, A. B., *Unequal Shares*, op. cit., p. 127.

21. Pond *et al.*, op. cit., p. 16.

22. Atkinson, op. cit., p. 126.

23. Pond *et al.*, op. cit., p. 17.

24. Kay and King, op. cit., p. 162.

25. Sandford, C. T., Willis, J. R. M. and Ironside, D. J., *An Accessions Tax*, IFS, 1973.

26. See Sandford C. T., 'The Wealth Tax Debate' in Field, F. (ed.), *The Wealth Report*, Routledge & Kegan Paul, 1979.

12. Home-made Socialism

1. *Social Insurance and Allied Services*, op. cit., p. 166.
2. ibid., pp. 165–6.
3. ibid., p. 166.
4. Marwick, A., 'The Labour Party and the Welfare State in Britain 1900–1948', op. cit.
5. Marwick, A., 'Middle Opinion in the Thirties', *English Historical Review*, April 1964.
6. Addison, P., *The Road to 1945*, Cape, 1975.
7. *Hansard*, 16 February 1943, col. 1623–4.
8. *Social Insurance: Workmen's Compensation and the NHS*, Labour Party, 1945, p. 5.
9. Donaghue, B. and Jones, G. W., *Herbert Morrison, Portrait of a Politician*, Weidenfeld & Nicholson, 1973, p. 325.
10. Cooke, C., *The Life of Richard Stafford Cripps*, Hodder & Stoughton, 1959, p. 322.
11. Attlee, C., *The Granada Historical Records Interview*, Panther, 1967.
12. Williams, F., *A Prime Minister Remembers*, Heinemann, 1961, p. 56.
13. ibid., p. 57.
14. Attlee, C., *As It Happened*, Adams, nd, p. 154.
15. Shinwell, E., *Conflict Without Malice*, Odhams, 1955, pp. 158–9.
16. Dalton Diaries, unpublished manuscript, LSE Library, entry dated 18 February 1943. I am grateful to the British Library of Politics and Economic Science for permission to reprint this quotation.
17. Wilson, H., *The Labour Government, 1964–1970: A Personal View*, Weidenfeld & Nicolson and Michael Joseph, 1971.
18. See Field, F., 'Killing a Commitment', *New Society*, 17 June 1976.

Appendix II: Back to Beveridge

1. The latest is *Over-ruled on Welfare*, Hobart Paperback no. 13, IEA, 1979.
2. Atkinson, A. B., *Poverty in Britain and the Reform of Social Security*, Cambridge University Press, 1969, p. 188.

3. Beveridge Report, op. cit., para. 12, quoted in Lister, R., *Social Security: The Case for Reform*, CPAG, 1975.
4. Report of a committee chaired by Professor J. E. Meade, *The Structure and Reform of Direct Taxation*, Institute of Fiscal Studies and George Allen & Unwin, 1978, p. 294.
5. *Beyond Beveridge*, The Outer Circle Policy Unit, 1978, p. 60.
6. Parker, H., *Goodbye Beveridge?*, Outer Circle Policy Unit, 1980, p. 46.

Index

Edward Shorter

THE MAKING OF
THE MODERN FAMILY

How has marriage changed over the past three centuries? Is the nuclear family disintegrating, and why? Has women's new freedom affected the traditional sexual balance? And what is the role of children in the family, past and present?

In this remarkable history of the family in Western society, Edward Shorter draws on a wide range of research into such areas as courtship, illegitimacy, child care, sexual practices, family planning, and the sharing of household responsibilities. He describes not only changes in structure, but changes in how people, rich and poor, thought and felt about themselves. He shows how the Victorian 'sexualization' of marriage contributed to the development of the enclosed nuclear family, and suggests that in the future the couple, rather than the family, may be the key unit.

'a compulsively readable book'   J. H. Plumb

'the material . . . is irresistible'   Jonathan Raban

'vivid, admirably digested, immensely lively and full of ideas'
New Statesman

'A most important contribution to historical understanding'
The Times Literary Supplement

INTO UNKNOWN ENGLAND 1866-1913

SELECTIONS FROM THE SOCIAL EXPLORERS

Edited by Peter Keating

How did the poor live in late Victorian and Edwardian England? In the slums of London and Birmingham? In the iron-town of Middlesbrough? In a Devon fishing village? In rural Essex?

This is a fascinating sequence of extracts from the writings of those individuals, journalists and wealthy businessmen, a minister's wife, and a popular novelist, who temporarily left the comfort of their middle-class homes to find out how the other half lived. Peter Keating includes material from Charles Booth, Jack London, B. S. Rowntree and C. F. G. Masterman as well as by such lesser-known figures as George Sims, Andrew Mearns and Stephen Reynolds.

'. . . a brilliant and compelling anthology . . . *Into Unknown England* is not only an education in itself, throwing into three-dimensional chiaroscuro the flat statistics of "scientific" history, but a splendid example of prose which is always immediate and alive.'
Alan Brien, *Spectator*

'The writers collected here used all the techniques they could to solicit sympathy. Their descendants are a thousand television documentaries.'
Paul Barker, *The Times*

'. . . a rich collection of passages, intelligently presented.'
The Guardian